Famous Chinese Gardens

中國名園

（纪念版）

陳從周
Chen Congzhou

同济大学出版社　上海

陈从周先生百年诞辰纪念

Commemorating the Centenary of Chen Congzhou's Birth

2018 年，因中国著名古典园林与建筑艺术家陈从周先生的百年诞辰而非同寻常。

为了这份特别的纪念，我们将陈从周先生的四部经典学术著作《苏州园林》《苏州旧住宅》《扬州园林（与住宅）》《中国名园》汇集再版。文字的重新录入与勘校，照片、测绘图的重新查找与制作……我们倾注满腔心血，将崇敬之情融入每段文字、每张图片的编排与设计之中。

为了明晰文字内容与图片之间的逻辑关系，我们在忠于原书稿素材的基础上，重新调整了图文次序，并对四本书中的照片和测绘图较原版做了局部删减。另外，因新寻找到陈从周先生当年拍摄的扬州园林照片，《扬州园林与住宅》（原《扬州园林》）较原版做了约 50 张图片的增补。

由于汇集再版的四部著作的原版来自不同的年代、不同的英文译者、不同的出版社，因此译文风格与专有名词译法迥异。加之目前园林等专有名词尚未有统一的官方译法（政府部门、景点官网、国际组织、民间等各方的译法不一），作为"纪念版"，为了尽量保持原版的历史风貌与体系完整，对于专有名词的英译，我们只做了所属书内的统一。

四部久负盛名的经典著作，再现一位建筑前辈的魁奇风骨。

——编者按

2018 is a very special year because of the centenary of a great man in the field of Chinese architecture.

To memorize the extraordinary significance, we are going to republish Mr. Chen's four classic academic works: *Suzhou Gardens*, *Traditional Suzhou Residences*, *Yangzhou Gardens (and Traditional Residences)*, and *Famous Chinese Gardens*. We have put great effort into these books, typing and proofreading texts, collecting photos and drawings, editing images... We designed and arranged the layout and pictures with the highest respect for the author.

While trying our best to maintain the authenticity of the contents, we have adjusted the sequence of the contents and deleted some photos and drawings compared to the original, so as to better clarify the relationship between texts and pictures. In addition, due to the newly discovered photos of Yangzhou gardens taken by the author, about 50 pictures in *Yangzhou Gardens and Traditional Residences* (originally *Yangzhou Gardens*) were added.

Since the original editions of the four reprinted works are from different time, translated by different translators into English, and published by different publishers, the translation styles are not alike, and the proper nouns are translated in different ways. Currently, there is no unified official translation for the proper nouns. For example, for gardens, government departments, official websites of the scene spots, international organizations, and the general public have their own English translations. As the four books published this time are "Centenary Edition", the original historical features and complete system of which should be maintained as much as possible, we have only made the translations of proper nouns consistent within each book.

The four classic works on classical Chinese gardens and residences are revived, reflecting the distinguished character of a trailblazing Chinese architectural master.

— The Editors

目录 | Table of Contents

園日涉以成趣

中国园林如画如诗，集建筑、书画、文学、园艺等艺术的精华，在世界造园艺术中独树一帜。

每一个园都有自己的风格。游颐和园，印象最深的应是昆明湖与万寿山；游北海，则是湖面与琼华岛。苏州拙政园曲折弥漫的水面、扬州个园峻拔的黄石大假山等，都同样令人印象深刻。

在造园时，如能利用天然的地形再加人工的设计配合，不但可以节约人工物力，而且利于景物的安排，造园学上称之为"因地制宜"。

An Interest in a Garden Grows with Daily Visits

Chinese gardens, both picturesque and lyrical, distinguish themselves from other gardens in the world by successfully integrating architecture, paintings, calligraphy and literature with garden design.

Each classical Chinese garden has its own unique style. Yihe Garden (the Summer Palace) impresses visitors with Kunming Lake and Wanshou Hill (Longevity Hill); Beihai Park attracts visitors with the ripples on the lake and Qionghua Islet; Zhuozheng Garden in Suzhou is noted for its winding and misty streams and Geyuan Garden in Yangzhou for its precipitous yellow stone cliffs.

In designing a garden, it is desirable to take full advantage of the natural features of a location to save labor and materials; but it is more important to integrate these features with the garden itself. This is known as "to adapt your design to nature" in gardening.

Some Chinese gardens give priority to hills and some others to water. There are also gardens that emphasize hills with water as complementary scenery and gardens that highlight water with hills as supplementary views. Bodies of water are either gathered or distributed around the gardens while the hills look either plain or precipitous. Gardens excel in scenery and the scenery varies from garden to garden. Each of these gardens proclaims its own unique style. To appreciate them, visitors may take delight in having an in-position or in-motion view, that is, to view them from a fixed position or by simply wandering about. But while

借景玉泉山
| Borrowing the scenery from Yuquan Hill

颐和园
| The Summer Palace

颐和园原为慈禧太后的夏宫。每到夏日，荷花盛放，衬以蓝天白云、
黄瓦红墙，一派辉煌气象。

The Summer Palace used to be a summer resort for Empress Dowager
Cixi. It looks magnificently alluring in summer when lotus flowers are
in full blossom against the blue sky, yellow tiles and red walls.

中国园林有以山为主体的，有以水为主体的，也有以山为主、以水为辅的，或以水为主、以山为辅的。而水亦有散、聚之分，山有平冈、峻岭之别。园以景胜，景因园异，各具风格。在观赏时，又有动观与静观之趣。因此，评价某一园林艺术时，要看它是否发挥了这一园景的特色，不落常套。

中国古典园林绝大部分四周皆有墙垣，景物藏于内。然而，园外有些景物还要组合到园内来，使空间推展极远，予人以不尽之意，此即所谓"借景"。颐和园借近处的玉泉山和较远的西山之景，每当夕阳西下时，在湖山真意亭处凭栏，二山仿佛移置园中，确是妙法。

中国园林，往往在大园中包小园，如颐和园的谐趣园、北海的静心斋、拙政园的枇杷园、留园的揖峰轩等，它们不但给园林以开朗或收敛的不同境界，同时又巧妙地把大小不同、结构各异的建筑物与山、石、树木安排

reflecting on the art of a garden, visitors should pay attention to whether or not the garden has made good use of the surrounding scenery, for this is what makes Chinese gardens so unusual.

Most classical Chinese gardens are surrounded by walls that harbor the scenery inside. However, the scenery inside the gardens should be complemented by the scenery from outside in order to stretch the space far beyond and to evoke a sense of infinity. This is what is known as "borrowing scenery". For instance, the famous garden of the Summer Palace serves as a good example of borrowing both the scenery of nearby Yuquan Hill and the scenery from faraway West Hill. A view from Hushanzhenyi Pavilion at sunset evokes a fantasy of the two hills being moved into the garden.

It is common for Chinese gardens to feature small gardens inside a large one, such as Xiequ Garden inside the Summer Palace, Jingxin Chapel inside Beihai Park, Pipa Garden inside Zhuozheng Garden and Yifeng Gallery inside Liuyuan Garden. This unique feature unites both the spacious and compact dimensions and keeps buildings of different sizes and structures in harmony with the hills and rocks, trees and flowers. Santanyinyue (Three Ponds Mirroring the Moon) inside the West Lake skillfully illustrates the technique of large lakes encircling small ones. These small gardens and lakes are, more often than not, the essence of gardens. The layout of buildings, the piling up of hills and rocks and the arrangement of potted landscape are all made with such exquisite craftsmanship that goes well beyond one's imagination. When visiting the gardens, it is advisable to view the small scenes in an in-position way, that is, while standing still, for such

小径月门别有洞天
| A path through the moon gate under moonlight

得恰到好处。至于大湖中包小湖的办法，要推西湖的三潭印月最妙了。这些小园、小湖多数是园中精华所在，无论在建筑处理，还是山石堆叠、盆景配置等，都是细笔工描，耐人寻味。游园的时候，对于这些小境界，宜静观盘桓。这与廊引人随的动观看景适成相反。

中国园林的景物主要模仿自然，用人工的力量来建造天然的景色，即所谓"虽由人作，宛自天开"。这些景物虽不一定强调仿自某山某水，但多少有些根据，用精炼概括的手法重现，颐和园的仿西湖便是一例，妙在与西湖的不尽相同。亦有利用山水画的画稿，参以诗词的情调，构成许多诗情画意的景色，在曲折多变的景物中，还运用了对比和衬托等手法。颐和园前山为华丽的建筑群，后山却是苍翠的自然景物，两者予人不同的感觉，相得益彰。在中国园林中，往往以建筑物与山石作对比，大与小作对比，高与低作对比，疏与密作对比，

still views form a contrast with views that visitors get in an in-motion way, that is, while lingering along open walkways that lead them forward without a stop.

The various scenes in Chinese gardens imitate natural landscapes. This artistic approach is known as "looking natural though man-made". Although these scenes are not necessarily copied from a specific hill or lake, they are nevertheless reproduced in a way that loosely resembles the real object. Although the Mirorr West Lake in the Summer Palace was built to mirror the West Lake, they do not entirely look alike. Many of the poetic and picturesque scenes in the gardens are created to look like the famous Chinese mountain-and-water paintings that are coupled by sentimental feelings in poems.

Contrast and balance are used to build winding and graceful scenes in Chinese gardens. In the Front Hill area of the Summer Palace, a complex of magnificent buildings offers a dramatic contrast with the natural, dense and green scenery in the Rear Hill area. These scenes project a series of integrated images to the viewers. Chinese gardens are characterized by an elegant balance between architecture and hills and rocks, big and small, high and low, and sparse and dense. The main scene in a garden is highlighted by the minor scenes to make a distinction between the dominating and supporting roles they play in the garden, as illustrated by the White Pagoda in Beihai Park, the Five Pavilions in Jingshan Garden, and Foxiang Tower in the Summer Palace.

In Chinese gardens, in addition to the arrangement of hills and rocks, trees and flowers, it is vital to have an ingenious setting for architecture; for example, to hide a tower in

北海白塔
| The White Pagoda in Beihai Park

恭王府萃锦园诗画舫
| Shihua Boat in Cuijin Garden of Prince Gong's Mansion

北京恭王府是中国现存最完整的一所王府花园，建筑风格凝重华丽，是北
方古典园林中的佳作。

Prince Gong's Mansion in Beijing is the best preserved imperial garden in
China, where buildings feature solemn and magnificent architectural styles,
demonstrating a masterpiece among classical gardens in the north of China.

等等。而一园的主要景物又由若干次要的景物衬托而出，使宾主分明，像北京北海的白塔、景山的五亭、颐和园的佛香阁便是。

中国园林，除山、石、树木外，建筑物的巧妙安排十分重要，如花间隐榭、水边安亭，还可利用长廊云墙、曲桥漏窗等构成各种画面，使空间更加扩大，层次分明。因此，游过中国园林的人会感到庭园虽小，却曲折有致。这就是景物组合成不同的空间感觉，有开朗、有收敛、有幽深、有明畅。游园观景，如看中国画的长卷一样，次第接于眼帘，观之不尽。

"好花须映好楼台"。到过北海团城的人，没有一个不说团城承光殿前的松柏布置得妥帖宜人。这是什么道理？其实是松柏的姿态与附近的建筑物高低相称，又利用了"树池"将它参差散植，加以适当的组合，使疏密有致，掩映成趣。苍翠虬枝与红墙碧瓦构成一幅极好的画面，怎不令人

flowers and to erect a pavilion by water. Long corridors, undulating walls, winding bridges and lattice windows may also be employed to further enlarge the space and to bring distinctive multi-layers to scenes. Therefore, those who tour Chinese gardens find them full of variety in the overall layout albeit their small sizes. Here the integration of scenes and objects gives rise to different effects in space: sometimes open and sometimes secluded; deep and serene here, and clear and lucid there. Visiting Chinese gardens is much like appreciating a long scroll of Chinese painting, as beautiful views come into sight one after another endlessly.

"Beautiful flowers are planted to grace beautiful pavilions." Those who have been to Tuancheng in Beihai Park are all impressed by the pleasingly appropriate arrangement of the pines and cedars in front of Chengguang Hall in Tuancheng. Why can it achieve such an effect? For one thing, the various shapes of pines and cedars go well with the neighboring buildings in height; for another, the pines and cedars are separately planted among a Pool of Trees in proper combination and density. The harmonious relationship between plants and buildings adds more interest to the scenery. Emerald green curly branches against red walls and bluish green tiles create strikingly graceful views. How can visitors resist not returning to the garden to further admire its beauty? In a similar vein, the crab apple trees in front of Leshou Hall in the Summer Palace form an exquisite and splendid view against the background of covered walkways. These are all masterpieces of making good use of plants in gardens. In gardens in the southern ranges of Changjiang River, a distinctively unique style is formed by planting flowers and trees that are rich and colorful, as well as bamboos and stones that are clear and tall, against the setting of white

圆明园遗址
| Remains of Yuanmingyuan Garden

有"万园之园"美誉的圆明园毁于英法联军之兵火，原仿江南园林的景色已不复见，只余西洋楼和大水法等欧洲式建筑的残柱遗基。
Yuanmingyuan Garden, well known as "Garden of Gardens" was burned down by the Anglo-French Allied Forces. The original imitations of the scenery south of Changjiang River are no longer in existence. All remains today are the broken walls and shattered stones of the European style buildings such as Xiyanglou and Dashuifa.

流连忘返呢？颐和园乐寿堂前的海棠同样与四周的廊屋形成了玲珑绚烂的构图，这些都是绿化中的佳作。江南的园林利用白墙作背景，配以华滋的花木、清拔的竹石，明洁悦目，别具一格。园林中的花木大都是经过长期的修整，使姿态曲尽画意。

园林中除假山外，尚有立峰，这些单独欣赏的佳石，如抽象的雕刻品，欣赏时往往以情悟物，进而将它人格化，称其"人峰""圭峰"之类。它必具有"瘦、皱、透、漏"的特点，方称佳品，即要玲珑剔透。中国古代园林中，要有佳峰珍石，方称得上"名园"。上海豫园的玉玲珑、苏州留园的冠云峰，在太湖石[1]中都是上选，使园林生色不少。

若干园林亭阁，不但有很好的命名，有时还加上很好的对联。读过刘鹗的《老残游记》，总还记得老残在济南游大明湖，看了"四面荷花三面柳，一城山色半城湖"的对联后，暗

walls. Most flowers and trees in these gardens are trimmed into lyrical and flowing shapes.

Peaks are erected in addition to rockeries in the gardens. Rockeries of fine stones with tall peaks are to be appreciated alone, just like abstract sculptures. In cherishing them, visitors cannot help understanding them with much affection; and therefore personifying them unconsciously and naming them Human Peak, Jade Tablet Peak and the like. A fine stone is characterized by being slim, wrinkled, transparent and perforate. That is, it must be exquisite and as clear as a crystal. In gardens of ancient China, a garden could only become famous by having fine peaks and precious stones in it. Yulinglong Jade Stone in Yuyuan Garden in Shanghai and Guanyun Peak in Liuyuan Garden in Suzhou are made of the best Taihu stones[1], adding luster to these gardens.

Some pavilions in gardens are not only given nice names but also complimented with well written couplets. Those who have read *Travels of Lao Can* by Liu E may well remember that Lao Can couldn't help saying to himself "What a view!" during his trip around Daming Lake in Jinan when he saw the couplet that read "against the background of lotus flowers and willows, the city is trimmed by mountains and lakes". This example demonstrates the important role that literature plays in gardens.

Gardens present different scenes in different seasons. As Guo Xi, a well-known mountain-and-water painter in the Northern Song Dynasty wrote in his review on paintings of *Linquangaozhi*: hills in spring are light and merry as if smiling; hills in summer are green and verdant as if sprouting; hills in autumn are bright and clear as if wearing make-up; hills in winter are pale and still as if sleeping.

苏州沧浪亭
| Canglang Pavilion in Suzhou

粉墙疏影、洞门曲户是江南园林建筑风格，与北地住宅形式大相径庭。
It is typical to have shadows on white-washed walls and perforated
windows inside arched doors in garden residences in the south of
Changjiang River, which forms a sharp contrast with the architectural styles
of residences in the north of China.

暗称道："真个不错。"可见文学在园林中所起的作用。

不同的季节，园林呈现不同的风光。北宋山水画名家郭熙在其画论《林泉高致》中说过："春山淡冶而如笑，夏山苍翠而如滴，秋山明净而如妆，冬山惨淡而如睡。"造园者多少参用了这些画理，扬州的个园便是用了春、夏、秋、冬四季不同的假山。在色泽上，春山用略带青绿的石笋；夏山用灰色的湖石；秋山用褐色的黄石；冬山用白色的雪石。黄石山奇峭凌云，俾便秋日登高。雪石罗堆厅前，冬日可作居观，便是体现这个道理。晓色春开，春随人意，游园当及时。

To some extent these principles of paintings have been deployed by garden designers. Geyuan Garden in Yangzhou is a case in point where rockeries for spring, summer, autumn and winter are placed. In terms of color and luster, the spring rockery is made of slightly blue-green stalagmite; the summer rockery of grey lake stones; the autumn rockery of brown yellow stones; and the winter rockery of white snow stones. Consequently, visitors tend to climb up the yellow stone rockery in autumn for its lofty peaks that reach into the clouds, and to reside in the garden for appreciation of the snow stones which are piled up in front of the hall in winter.

Visitors should lose no time to visit gardens when they are in a good mood with the coming of spring.

注释：

1. 太湖石产于中国江苏省太湖区域，是一种多孔而玲珑剔透的石头，多用以点缀庭院，是建造中国园林不可缺少的材料之一。

Notes:

1. Taihu stones are produced in the area of Taihu Lake of Jiangsu Province, China. They are ingeniously perforated natural stones mainly used for decorating courtyards as indispensible building materials for Chinese gardens.

南京瞻园小景
| A view at Zhanyuan Garden in Nanjing

悠然把酒對西山

颐和园

"更喜高楼明月夜，悠然把酒对西山"，明米万钟[1] 在他北京西郊的园林里写了这两句诗，一望而知是从晋人陶渊明"采菊东篱下，悠然见南山"脱胎而来的。不管"对"也好，"见" 也好，所指的都是远处的山，这就是中国园林设计中的"借景"，即把远景纳为园中一景，增加该园的景色变化。这在中国古代造园中早已应用，明计成[2] 在他所著《园冶》一书中总结出来，才有了定名。他所说"借者，园虽别内外，得景无拘远近"，已阐述得很明白了。

One Gazes Leisurely at the West Hill over Wine
—The Summer Palace

"On a night full of moonlight, it is enjoyable to gaze at the West Hill over wine from a tower." These are the lines written by Mi Wanzhong[1] in his garden in the western outskirts of Beijing during the Ming Dynasty. Obviously these lines were composed after the well-known lines of Tao Yuanming in the Jin Dynasty. "As I pick chrysanthemums beneath the eastern fence, my eyes fall leisurely on the Southern Mountain." No matter whether the action is "to gaze at" or "to fall on", what one can see are the mountains in the distance. This is what is referred to as "borrowing scenery" in Chinese garden design. To include distant scenery as a part of a garden adds variety to landscapes in the garden. This technique, which was initially invented and practiced in Chinese garden design in ancient times, was then given a proper name in *The Craft of Gardens* by Ji Cheng[2] in the Ming Dynasty. He made it explicitly clear when he said, "To borrow from the scenery means that as long as there is a good view, one should try to borrow it without being bothered by whether it is close or far away, even though the interior of a garden is distinct from what lies outside it." [3]

It is ideal to establish gardens in the western outskirts of Beijing where the West Hill tops stretch along to form screens and streams converge to become lakes. This site in Beijing has witnessed a collection of beautiful gardens in history, especially during the Ming and Qing dynasties, among which Yuanmingyuan Garden is well known as the Garden of Gardens.

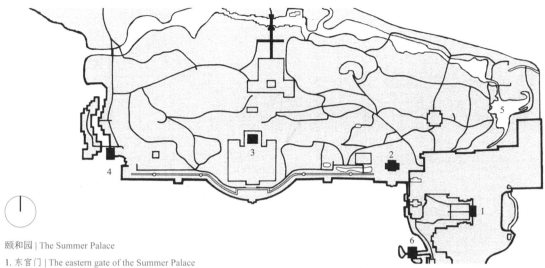

颐和园 | The Summer Palace

1. 东宫门 | The eastern gate of the Summer Palace
2. 乐寿堂 | Leshou Hall
3. 佛香阁 | Foxiang Tower
4. 石舫 | Marble Boat
5. 谐趣园 | Xiequ Garden
6. 知春亭 | Zhichun Pavilion

颐和园东宫门晨雾
| Morning in the mist at the eastern gate of the Summer Palace

北京的西郊，西山蜿蜒若屏，清泉汇为湖沼，最宜建园，历史上曾为北京园林集中之地。明清两代，园林蔚为大观，其中圆明园更被称为"万园之园"。

圆明园这座在历史上驰名中外的园林，其于造园之术，可用"因水成景，借景西山"八个字来概括。圆明园的成功在于"因""借"二字，是中国古代园林主要造园手法的具体表现。偌大的一个园林，如果立意不明，终难成佳构；所以，造园要立意在先，尤其是郊园。郊园多野趣，重借景。以上两点不论中国传统的哪一个园都能体现出来。

圆明园在 1860 年英法联军入侵北京时被兵火所焚，仅存断垣残基。如今，只能用另一个大园林——颐和园来谈借景。

颐和园在北京西北郊十公里处。万寿山耸翠园北，昆明湖弥漫山前，玉泉山蜿蜒其西，风景洵美。

Yuanmingyuan Garden has been renowned both at home and abroad throughout history. The art of its landscape design can be best captured by "creating scenery from following waters and borrowing the scenery from the West Hill". The success of Yuanmingyuan Garden lies in its "following" and "borrowing from" the existing scenery, which manifests two of the key principles of landscape design in China in ancient times. This garden is so large that it could never have become a masterpiece without a theme. Therefore, it is of primary importance to give priority to the creation of a theme in landscape design of very large gardens. This is especially true with gardens on the outskirts of a city which emphasize keeping the wildness of nature and borrowing from the existing scenery. These two principles are practised in every classical garden in China, e. g. in the Summer Palace.

Yuanmingyuan Garden was mercilessly burnt down when Beijing was invaded by the united forces of the Great Britain and France in 1860 , and all that remains today are broken walls and shattered stones. But for now, we cannot but use the Summer Palace, another grand-scale garden, as an example to illustrate the principle of borrowing the scenery.

The Summer Palace lies 10 km northwest of Beijing, inside which Longevity Hill stands on the north side of the garden. The landscape is remarkably beautiful with the mist from Kunming Lake pervading in front of the hill and with Yuquan Hill stretching continuously along the west of the Summer Palace.

The Summer Palace (Yihe Garden) was named Wengshan Jinhai (Graceful Mountain and Golden Sea) in the Yuan Dynasty and was renamed

颐和园长廊

| The Long Corridor in the Summer Palace

长廊循万寿山南麓沿昆明湖北岸构筑，长 728 米。藻井枋梁上绘有
苏式彩画。游人漫步廊中，既可欣赏廊内精美彩画，又可浏览廊外
湖光山色。

The 728-meter long Long Corridor starts from the southern foot of
Longevity Hill and winds along the northern bank of Kunming Lake.
There are colored drawings of Suzhou style on the ceilings and beams
of the corridor. While wandering along the corridor, visitors may both
admire the fine drawings along the corridor and appreciate the beautiful
scenery of mountains and lakes beyond the corridor.

颐和园万寿山
| Longevity Hill in the Summer Palace

万寿山前临昆明湖，佛香阁高踞山巅。自山脚的牌楼经排云殿、德
辉殿、佛香阁，直至山顶的智慧海，形成一条层层上升的中轴线——
这巨大的主体建筑群为全园的精华所在。

Longevity Hill faces Kunming Lake with Foxiang Tower perched on the
hill top. A huge complex of magnificent buildings along an ascending
central axis remains the highlights of the Palace: Pailou (the Cermonial
Gateway) at the foot of the hill, Paiyun Hall, Dehui Hall, Foxiang Tower
and Zhihuihai Hall at the top of the hill.

颐和园在元代名"瓮山金海"，至明代有所增饰，名"好山园"，清康熙四十一年（1702）曾就此作瓮山行宫。清乾隆十五年（1750）开始大规模兴建，更名"清漪园"。1860年为英法联军所毁，1886年修复，易名"颐和园"，1900年又为八国联军所破坏，1903年又重修，遂成今状。

颐和园是以杭州西湖为蓝本，精心模拟，故西堤、水岛、烟柳画桥，皆移江南的淡妆，现北地之胭脂，景虽有相同，趣则各异。

园面积达三四平方公里，水面占四分之三，"北国江南"因水而成。入东宫门，见仁寿殿，峻宇翚飞，峰石罗前，绕其南豁然开朗，明湖在望。

万寿山面临昆明湖，佛香阁踞其巅，八角四层，俨然为全园之中心。

Haoshan Garden (Good Mountain Garden) following its further embellishment in the Ming Dynasty In the forty-first year of the Kangxi reign (1702) in the Qing Dynasty, the garden became Wengshan Xinggong (Temporary Imperial Garden Residence). In the fifteenth year of the Qianlong reign (1750) in the Qing Dynasty, the garden residence was further expanded and renamed again as Qingyi Garden (Garden of Clear Ripples). Then in 1860, the garden was burnt down by the allied forces of the Great Britain and France. Twenty-six years later in 1886, the garden was reconstructed and given its modern name of Yihe Garden (Garden of Good Health and Harmony). Unfortunately it was destroyed again by the Eight-Power Allied Forces in 1900. Another reconstruction was completed in 1903 and has lasted to this day.

Meticulously imitating the landscape of the West lake in Hangzhou, the Summer Palace has a layout featured in Xidi (West Causeway), islets, misty willows and picturesque bridges, as if wearing the light make-up of China south of Changjiang River and the rouge of the north of China. The landscapes here reveal different tastes albeit their similarities.

The Summer Palace covers an area between three and four square kilometers, of which about three-fourths are covered by water, revealing its similarity to the landscape south of Changjiang River. Upon entering the eastern gate of the Palace, visitors may catch sight of Renshou Hall with its shooting cornices and precipitous stones in the front. Going round the hall to its southern end, visitors will be led unexpectedly into an open vastness of a clear lake.

十七拱桥上的石狮
| Stone lions on the Seventeen-Arch Bridge

登阁则西山如黛，湖光似镜，跃入眼帘；俯视则亭馆扑地，长廊萦带。景色全囿于一园之内，其所以得无尽之趣，在于借景。小坐湖畔的湖山真意亭，玉泉山山色塔影移入槛前，而西山不语，直走京畿，明秀中又富雄伟，为他园所不及。

廊在中国园林中极尽变化之能事，颐和园长廊可算显例，其予游者之兴味最浓，印象特深。廊引人随，中国画山水手卷于此舒展，移步换影。上苑别馆，有别宫禁，宜其清代帝王常作园居。

谐趣园独自成区，倚万寿山之东麓，积水以成池，周以亭榭，小桥浮水，游廊随径，适宜静观——此大园中之小园，自有天地。该园仿江南无

Foxiang Tower rises majestically on top of Longevity Hill which faces Kunming Lake. The tower, which has a majestic octagonal roof and towering four stories, becomes the center of the garden. When visitors climb the tower on the hilltop, they feel enchanted by the silhouette of the West Hill and by the beautiful lake which shines like a mirror; when they look down, they see pavilions with long winding corridors. They feel overjoyed for being able to enjoy a multitude of views from just one garden, and this is attributable to the concept of borrowing from the scenery. When visitors sit down in Hushanzhenyi Pavilion by the lake, the beautiful scenery of Yuquan Hill come into view. Meanwhile, the West Hill tops lead quietly into the city, adding greater grandeur to the elegance of the view.

The covered walkways in Chinese gardens excel in their changing views. A good example of this is the Long Corridor of the Summer Palace, the beauty of which is truly astonishing. This corridor leads one to a wide range of Chinese scroll paintings and as the view of these scroll paintings unfolds along the corridor, the view changes with each step a visitor takes. The gardens and buildings here are distinctive from those around the palace, which made them more attractive to emperors in the Qing Dynasty for their summer time.

At the eastern foot of Longevity Hill lies Xiequ Garden which is a park in itself. Small streams converge to form a pond in Xiequ Garden; pavilions stand by the pond, bridges over it and covered walkways wind along foot paths, creating unique in-position views that visitors may appreciate better when standing still. This small garden inside the big garden of the Summer Palace is an imitation of Jichang Garden in Wuxi

从知春亭望万寿山
| A view of Longevity Hill from Zhichun Pavilion

锡寄畅园，以同属山麓园，故有积水，皆有景可借。

水曲由岸，水隔因堤，故颐和园以长堤分隔，斯景始出。而桥式之多，构图之美，处处画本，若玉带桥之莹洁柔和，十七孔桥之仿佛垂虹。每逢山横春霭，新柳拂水，游人泛舟所得之景与陆上所得之景分明异趣，而处处皆能映西山入园，足证"借景"之妙。

south of Changjiang River. Both gardens are built at the foot of hills with water around and with surrounding scenery available to be borrowed beyond the gardens.

Streams are shaped by their winding bank and water are separated by dikes; consequently, the Summer Palace is divided by long embankments, thus givingrise to a variety of views. Bridges appeal to visitors because of their variety in the architectural styles and structures, which create views like beautiful Chinese paintings everywhere. For example, Yudai Bridge appears crystallized and gentle; and the Seventeen-Arch Bridge takes the shape of a rainbow. Whenever springmist floats from amid a hill and new willows touch the water, visitors in boats will find views from the water charmingly different from views from the land. The West Hill can be seen everywhere from inside the Summer Palace, which fully demonstrates the trick of "borrowing the scenery".

注释:

1. 米万钟（1570—1628 或 1631），中国明末的书画家，又为中国园林的著名设计师。现北京大学校园尚存的夕园即为米万钟创建的著名园林所在。

2. 计成是中国明末的园林学家，有著名的园林理论著作《园冶》传世。书成于 1631—1634 年间，总结了中国园林造园叠山的一套系统理论，对中国园林艺术的研究颇多建树。

Notes:

1. Mi Wanzhong (1570-1628 or 1631), a painter and a calligrapher in the late Ming Dynasty, was also known as a designer of landscapes. The existing Xiyuan Garden on the campus of Peking University was designed by him.

2. Ji Cheng was a designer of landscapes in the late Ming Dynasty. He finished composing, between 1631 and 1634, The Craft of Gardens, a masterpiece of garden design which was handed down from generation to generation. His theory of garden design in the Chinese tradition made great contributions to the research on the art of garden landscaping in China.

3. Translator's note: The quotation is from The Craft of Gardens translated by Alison Hardie(1998, Yale University Press: p.39).

由佛香阁俯视十七拱桥和南湖岛
| A bird's-eye view of the Seventeen-Arch Bridge and Nanhu Island from Foxiang Tower

谐趣园

| Xiequ Garden

颐和园著名的"园中之园"，富有江南情趣。

Xiequ Garden, rich in features of gardens south of Changjiang River, is
noted as the "garden inside gardens" of the Summer Palace.

移天缩地在君怀

避暑山庄

河北省承德市附近原为清帝狩猎的地方，骏马秋风，正是典型的北地风情。然而，承德避暑山庄这个著名的北方行宫苑囿却有杏花春雨般的江南景色，令人向往，游人到此总会流露出"谁云北国逊江南"的感叹。

苑囿之建，首在选址，需得山川之胜，辅以人工。重在选景，妙在点景，二美具而全景出。避暑山庄正得此妙谛。山庄群山环抱，武烈河自东北沿宫墙南下。有泉冬暖，故称"热河"。

清康熙于1703年始建山庄，经六年时间初步完成，作为离宫之用。

Miniaturized Heaven and Land Lie in Your Arms
—The Imperial Mountain Resort

Near the city of Chengde in Hebei Province, there used to be a hunting range for the emperors in the Qing Dynasty. This hunting area was typical of northern China where horses galloped against the autumn wind. However, Chengde Imperial Mountain Resort, known as the temporary imperial palace in the north, fascinates visitors with its alluring scenery characteristic of the south of Changjiang River as almond flowers flutter in the spring rain. Visitors cannot help feeling that "the north is not inferior to the south".

To build a garden, it is of top priority to select a site where the natural beauty of hills and water is to be supplemented with the work of man. A garden can only reach its uttermost beauty when it excels in both choosing the site and highlighting its surrounding scenery. This is best exemplified by Chengde Imperial Mountain Resort which is embraced by hills with Wulie River flowing along the palace wall from Rehe River.

The construction of the resort was initiated during the reign of Emperor Kangxi of the Qing Dynasty in 1703 and was preliminarily completed after six years. The resort, boasting its thirty-six scenic spots, was then served as a summer retreat which was known as the temporary imperial palace. Since this resort was established against the background of nature, it was given the name of Mountain Resort. Later in 1751, Chengde Imperial Mountain Resort was extended by the order of Emperor Qianlong, who further embellished the

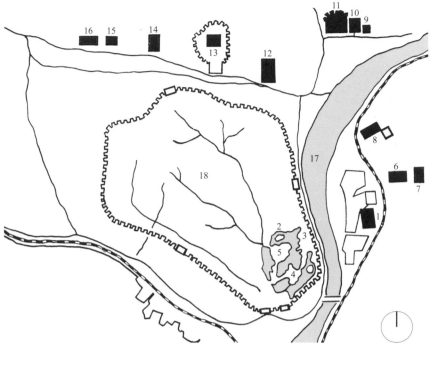

避暑山庄及其周边 | The Imperial Mountain Resort and its surrounding areas

1. 溥仁寺 | Puren Temple
2. 烟雨楼 | Yanyu Tower
3. 热河泉 | Rehe Spring
4. 月色江声 | Yuesejiangsheng
5. 如意洲 | Ruyi Islet
6. 普乐寺 | Pule Temple
7. 磐锤峰 | Qingchui Peak
8. 安远庙 | Anyuan Temple
9. 广缘寺 | Guangyuan Temple
10. 普佑寺 | Puyou Temple
11. 普宁寺 | Puning Temple
12. 须弥福寿之庙 | Xumifushou Temple
13. 普陀宗乘之庙 | Putuozongcheng Temple
14. 殊像寺 | Shuxiang Temple
15. 广安寺 | Guang'an Temple
16. 罗汉堂 | Luohan Hall
17. 武烈河 | Wulie River
18. 避暑山庄 | The Imperial Mountain Resort

宁谧的山庄清晨
| Tranquility at Dawn in the Mountain Resort

朴素无华，饶自然之趣，故以"山庄"名之，有三十六景。其后，乾隆又于1751年进行扩建，踵事增华，亭榭别馆骤增，遂又增三十六景。同时，建寺观，分布山区，规模较前益广。

行宫周约二十公里，多山岭，仅五分之一左右为平地，而平地又多水面，山岚水色，相映成趣。居住、朝会部分位于山庄之东。正门内为楠木殿，素雅不施彩绘，因所在地势较高，故近处湖光，远处岚影，可卷帘入户，借景绝佳。园区可分为两部分：东南之泉汇为湖泊；西北山陵起伏如带。林木茂而禽鸟聚，麋鹿散于丛中，鸣游自得。水曲因岸，水隔因堤，岛列其间，仿江南之烟雨楼、狮子林等，名园分绿，遂移北国。

山区建筑宜眺、宜憩，故以小巧出之而多变化。寺庙间列，晨钟暮鼓，

resort. Another thirty-six scenic spots were added to the garden along with many more pavilions and villas. Meanwhile, temples were set up in the mountains, expanding the resort to an unprecedented scale.

It extends as long as 20 km round this temporary imperial palace where there are an overwhelming number of mountains compared to plains which constitute only one-fifth of the total area and are mostly covered with water. The mountains and water complement the beauty of the palace which is composed of two areas: a living area and a garden area. The living area is situated in the east of the palace. Behind the front gate lies Nanmu Hall, which, with its subdued elegance, provides a perfect vantage point for visitors to appreciate the lake nearby and the mountain mist in the distance simply by rolling up the curtains, a perfect illustration of borrowing the scenery. The garden area can be divided into two parts: southwest and northwest. In the former springs flow into a lake whereas in the latter lie rolling mountain ranges. Deep woods provide shelters for birds and beasts such as *milu* deer, which can be spotted roaming in the trees. Amid the meandering river shaped by winding banks and dikes lie islands. which resemble Yanyu Tower and Shizilin Garden in the south. In this way beautiful scenery in famous gardens in the south is brought to the north.

Visitors enjoy looking far into the distance and taking relaxations at the pavilions and towers set in the mountains which are characterized by their being compact in size and different in styles. Here and there stand temples from where come the

避暑山庄外青葱山景
| The green moutainscape beyond the Imperial Mountain Resort

清 冷枚《避暑山庄图》

| Leng Mei (Qing Dynasty) *Painting of the Imperial Mountain Resort*

画幅长 254.8 cm，宽 172.5 cm。

Length: 254.8 cm, width: 172.5 cm.

锤峰落照

| Qingchui Peak at Sunset

"磬锤峰"为避暑山庄周围群山中的主峰，形似江南妇女洗衣用的
洗衣锤，故名。

Qingchui Peak is the main peak among the mountains surrounding the
Imperial Mountain Resort. It is named Chui after the pronunciation of
stick in Chinese, because it looks like a wash stick for women to wash
clothes in the south of China.

梵音到耳，且建藏书楼文津阁，储《四库全书》[1] 于此。园外，东北两面有外八庙，为极好的借景，融园内、园外之景为一。

山庄占地 5.64 平方公里，为现存苑囿中最大。山庄自然地势，有山岳平原与湖沼等，因地制宜，变化多端。而林木栽植，各具特征：山多松，间植枫；水边宜柳；湖中栽荷。园中"万壑松风""曲水荷香"皆因景而得名。而万树园中，榆树成林，浓荫蔽日，清风自来，有隔世之感。

中国苑囿之水，聚者为多，而避暑山庄湖沼得聚分之妙，其水自各山峪流下，东南经文园水门出，与武烈河相接。湖沼之中，安排如意洲、月色江声、芝径云堤、水心榭等洲、岛、桥、堰，分隔成东湖、如意洲湖及上、下湖区域。亭阁掩映，柳岸低迷，景深委婉。而山泉、平湖之水自有动静之分，故山麓有"暖流喧波""云容水态""远近泉声"；入湖沼则"澄

sounds of chanting in Sanskrit amid the morning bells and evening drumbeats. Wenjin Gallery, which is used to store books is located here. It has an entire collection of the Chinese classics called *Siku Quanshu*[1]. Seen from both the eastern and northern parts of the garden area, are the magnificent the Eight Outlying Temples, a superb example of borrowing the scenery by integrating scenes inside the garden area with those outside.

The resort, covering an area of 5.64 square kilometers, is the largest of all existing gardens. Its adaptation to the natural terrain of hills, flat areas, lakes and pools brings variety to its landscape. Trees and flowers are planted according to their nature: pines are placed in mountains, maples in valleys, willows by water and lotuses in lakes. Such scenic spots as the Valley of Pines and the Pond of Lotuses are named after the scenes in the garden. In the Garden of Ten-Thousand Trees, the dense elm woods provide soothing shade for visitors, who cannot help feeling carried away by the unearthly comfort of the cool breezes.

Bodies of water in Chinese gardens are typically gathered together; but lake and pools in Chengde Imperial Mountain Resort display a fine balance between being gathered and separated. Water flows from ravines through the water gate in the southeast part of Wenyan Garden into Wulie River. Islets, embankments and pavilions such as Ruyizhou Islet, Yuesejiangsheng, Zhijingyun Banks and Shuixin Pavilion in the lakes and pools divide the water naturally into the East Lake, Ruyizhou Lake, and Upper and Lower Lakes. With pavilions half-hidden in trees and rivers lined with weeping willows, the scenery evokes profound and

万树园

| Garden of Ten-Thousand Trees

在山庄平原区东北部。园内不施土木，按蒙古风俗设置蒙古包数座。
康熙、乾隆曾在此接见蒙古首领和西藏班禅六世等。

It lies in the northeast of the plain area in the Imperial Mountain Resort.
There are no buildings except a few Mongolian yurts in this garden.
Here Emperors Kangxi and Qianlong met the Mongolian leaders and the
sixth Panchen Lama from Tibet.

波叠翠""镜水云岭""芳渚临流"。水有百态，景存千变。

　　山庄按自然形势，广建亭台、楼阁、桥梁、水榭等，并且更就幽峪奇峰，建造寺观庵庙。东湖沼区域有金山寺、法林寺等。山岳区内，其数尤多，属道教者有广元宫、斗姥阁；属佛教者有珠源寺、碧峰寺、旃檀林、鹭云寺、水月庵等，有"内八庙"之称。殿阁参差，浮图隐现，朝霞夕月，梵音钟声，破寂静山林，绕神妙幻境。苑囿园林，于自然景物外，复与宗教建筑相结合。

　　山庄峰峦环抱，秀色可餐，隔武烈河遥望，有"锤峰落照"一景。自锤峰沿山而北，转狮子沟而西，依次建溥仁寺、溥善寺、普乐寺、安远庙、普佑寺、普宁寺、须弥福寿之庙、普陀宗乘之庙、殊像寺、广安寺、罗汉堂、狮子园等寺庙与别园，且分别模仿新疆、西藏等少数民族建筑造型，以及山海关以内各地建筑风格，崇巍瑰丽，与山庄建筑呼应争辉。试登离宫北部

sentimental feelings. The active mountain springs and still lakes create such different scenes. At the foot of the mountains, there are Warm Currents and Frolic Waves, Cloud Look and Water Form, and Sounds of Springs. On the lakes, visitors may also find Clear Waves in Green, Mirrored Water in Cloud Hills and Flowers by Water. Here water may take hundreds of shapes while scenes may display a myriad of changes.

There are a number of towers, multistoried-buildings, bridges and pavilions in the resort along with temples and nunneries in secluded ravines or on breathtaking peaks. In the East Lake area there are Jinshan Temple and Falin Temple. In the mountain area there are many more temples, including Taoist temples: Guangyuangong and Doulaoge; Buddhist temples and nunneries: Zhuyuan Temple, Bifeng Temple, Zhantanlin, Luyun Temple, and Shuiyue Nunnery. These Buddhist temples and nunneries are known as the Eight Inner Temples. All these buildings, together with the spectacular clouds, the moon, bell ringing and scripture recitations heard from the temples, make the resort a holy land, a harmonious coexistence of natural beauty and religious buildings. Amidst the towers and pavilions the chanting in Sanskrit and sound of bells from the temples and nunneries break the tranquility in the deep woods. At dawn or at dusk when the landscape looms in the distance with the moon above, one feels drawn into a fairyland. In addition to their marriage with the natural scenery, the gardens in the garden area are ingeniously integrated with the religious buildings.

Embraced by ridges and peaks, the Imperial Mountain Resort is blessed with beautiful scenery.

普陀宗乘之庙
| Putuozongcheng Temple

界墙之上，自东及北，诸庙尽入眼底，其与离宫几形成一空间整体，蔚为一大风景区。

用"移天缩地在君怀"这句话来概括山庄，可以说体现已尽。其能融南北园林于一处，组各民族建筑在一区，不觉其不协调、不顺眼，反觉面面有情，处处生景，实耐人寻味。故若正宫、月色江声等处实为北方民居四合院之组合方式，而万壑松风、烟雨楼等运用江南园林手法灵活布局。秀北雄南，目在咫尺，游人当可领略其造园之佳妙。

注释：

1. 《四库全书》是清代乾隆时期 1772—1782 年间编的一部大型丛书，内容广泛，保存并整理了大量中国古籍文献。全书共收古籍 3503 种，79 337 卷，分"经""史""子""集"四部，故名"四库全书"。

Across Wulie River is the well-known scenic spot of Qingchui Peak at Sunset. Going northward from the peak and then turning westward at Shizi Gully, visitors can see Puren, Pushan, Pule, Anyuan, Puyou, Puning, Xumifushou, Putuozongcheng, Shuxiang, Guang'an Temples, and Luohan Hall and Shizi Garden. All these buildings and the garden are designed to reflect the architectural styles of minority structures such as those in Xinjiang and Tibet as well as structures south of Shanhaiguan Pass. These sacred and magnificent buildings correspond with the buildings in the resort. From the north boundary wall of this summer imperial palace, visitors, looking from east to north, will recognize that the temples and pavilions in the distance have been harmoniously integrated with the buildings in the imperial palace.

"Miniaturized heaven and land lie in your arms"—this sentence can be said to be very comprehensive to summarize the characteristics of Imperial Mountain Resort, which combines the elements of southern and northern gardens, as well as the architecture of various ethnic groups. Visitors will be able to appreciate the exquisiteness of the garden art embodied in it.

Notes:

1. *Siku Quanshu*, compiled in the reign of Emperor Qianlong in the Qing Dynasty from 1772 to 1782, is a large-scale collection of works that covers a wide range of classical literature. The collection includes 3503 types of ancient books which are composed of 79 337 scrolls. The collection is named *Siku Quanshu*, the Complete Library in the Four Branches of Literature, for it is composed of four branches of "Jing", "Shi", "Zi" and "Ji".

金山

| Jinshan

康熙帝南巡，欣赏江苏镇江金山景物，故在山庄内仿造此景。正殿
三间，楼阁三层，是山庄湖区最高点。

Emperor Kangxi showed his admiration for the scenery at Jinshan,
Zhenjiang Town of Jiangsu Province on his inspection tour to the
south, which resulted in an imitated scenery of Jinshan in the Imperial
Mountain Resort. The three main pavilions, one of which being three-
storied, are the vantage point of the Lake Area in the resort.

烟雨楼
| Yanyu Tower

乾隆南巡，见浙江嘉兴烟雨楼景色秀美，于山庄内按图兴建。每当夏秋
之季，烟雨弥漫，仿如画中。

Impressed by the beautiful scenery at Yanyu Tower in Jiaxing, Zhejiang
Province on his inspection tour to the south, Emperor Qianlong had the
pavilion copied in the Mountain Resort based upon its plans. It looks lyrical
and picturesque when mist and rain fill the air in summer and autumn.

别有俚绵水石间

十笏园

山东潍坊十笏园是一座精巧得像水石盆景样的小园，占地二千多平方米，内有溶溶水石，楚楚楼台，其构思之妙，足为造小园之借鉴。

十笏园建于清光绪十一年（1885），原为丁善宝的园林。"笏"即朝笏，古代大臣朝见君王时所用，多以象牙制成。因园小巧玲珑，故以"十笏"名之。中国园林命名常存谦逊之意，如近园、半亩园、芥子园等皆此类。

园中以轻灵为胜，东筑假山，面山隔水为廊，廊尽渡桥，建水榭，旁列小筑，名"稳如舟"。临流有漪澜亭。池北花墙外为春雨楼，与池南倒座高下相向。

Water and Stones in a Garden Stir Emotions
—Shihu Garden

Shihu Garden in Weifang, Shandong Province is an exquisite miniature landscape of water and stones. Within an area of only about 2000 square meters, there are clusters of finely detailed pavilions and rockeries with water trickling through them. The garden is so ingeniously designed that it deserves to serve as a fine example for small gardens.

The Garden, built in the eleventh year of the Guangxu reign (1885), used to be a garden residence of Ding Shanbao. *Hu* was a formal thin board (used for note-keeping) made of ivory which cabinet members held in their hands when they had an audience with the emperor in ancient times. The garden was named *Shihu* (ten thin boards) to symbolize its tiny size. Chinese gardens are often named to indicate humbleness and modesty, as in the cases of Jinyuan Garden, Banmu Garden and Jiezi Garden.

The design of Shihu Garden highlights a feeling of ingenuity and lightness. In the eastern part of the garden stands a rockery. Across water lies a covered walkway, at the end of which sits a bridge. Near this bridge is a pavilion above water with a small house named Wenruzhou next to it. Yilan Pavilion is erected by the pond. Beyond an openwork wall north of the pond, Chunyu Tower stands tall in contrast to the low houses built in the southern part of the garden.

Pavilions, terraces, rockeries and stones sited by or into the pond stretch over water as if floating on ripples. The wonder of a water garden is dramatically enhanced by its small size. Therefore, it is not necessarily true that a mountain must be lofty to be majestic, and water boundless to create a perception of spaciousness.

十笏园假山及池中漪澜亭
| The Rockery and Yilan Pavilion in the pond in Shihu Garden

池东叠石成山，山上有二亭，登亭可瞰全园景色。池中漪澜亭与山上二亭互相呼应，三亭皆尺度合宜，小巧精致。
One may get a bird's-eye view of the garden from the two pavilions on top of the piled-up mountain to the east of the pond. Yilan Pavilion by the pond is integrated naturally with the two pavilions on the mountain. The three pavilions set in appropriate proportions illustrate ingenious design and exquisite craftsmanship.

亭台山石，临池仲水，如浮波上，得水园之妙，又能以小出之；故山不在高，水不在广，自有汪洋之意。而高大建筑，复隐其后，以隔出之，反现深远，而其紧凑蕴藉，耐人寻味者正在此。

小园用水，有贴水、依水之别。江苏吴江同里汪氏退思园，贴水园也。因同里为水乡，水位高，故该园山石、桥廊、建筑皆贴水面，予人之感如在水中央。苏州网师园，依水园也。亭廊依水而筑，因水位较低，故环池驳岸作阶梯状。同在水乡，其处理有异。然则园贴水、依水，除因水制宜外，更着眼于以有限之面积，化无限之水面。波光若镜，溪源不尽，能引人遐思。"盈盈一水间，脉脉不得语"——《古诗十九首》中境界，小园用水之极矣。

造大园固难，构小园亦不易。水为脉络，贯穿全园，而亭台山石，点缀出之，概括精练，如诗之绝句，词中小令，风韵神采即在此水石之间。北国有此明珠，亦巧运匠心矣。

On the contrary, tall buildings concealed behind the scenes evoke an impression of depth. The very mystery of the garden is embedded in its compactness and implicitness.

Water in a small garden can be used in two ways: structures can be placed above it or by it. Tuisi Garden of the Wang Family in Tongli of Wujiang, Jiangsu Province is a case in point. Because Tongli is a waterside town with a high water level, the rockeries, bridges, covered walkways and buildings in the garden are all constructed above the water, creating a feeling of standing in the center of the water. Wangshi Garden in Suzhou, on the other hand, exemplifies gardens by the water. Pavilions and corridors are built next to a pond and are arranged in a staircase-like style around the pond since the water level is low. Although these gardens are both located in waterside towns, different skills have been employed in balancing the relationship between buildings and nature. To design a garden above or by the water, the emphasis should be on creating an infinite watery expanse out of limited space. It inspires the imagination to have waves floating like mirrors and streams flowing endlessly from their sources. The brilliance of taking the most advantage of water in garden design is best captured by the enchanting imagery created in the lines from the *Nineteen Chinese Ancient Poems*: "Clear and clean water in between, my tender and tempting look at you dims my words."

It is challenging to build a large garden and the same is true with a small one. In a well-designed garden, waterways thread like veins through the garden which is dotted with pavilions, terraces, rockeries and stones. The arrangement is as concise as every move in classical Chinese poetry. The expressiveness of poems is found in compact lines; likewise, the charm of this garden lies in the refinement of water and stones. It is the ingenious design that accounts for this shining pearl in the north of China.

十笏园池中水榭
| Pavilions in the pond in Shihu Garden

十笏园布局以水池为中心，池中水榭四面临水，故用敞亭的形式，为园中第一佳景。

A pond is sited in the center of Shihu Garden. Open-sided pavilions in the pond are surrounded by the water, which makes the most alluring scenery in the garden.

绿杨宜作两家春

拙政园

"明月好同三径夜，绿杨直作两家春。"

拙政园现分为中、西两部。在西部补园，望隔院楼台，隐现花墙之上，欲去无从。登假山巅的宜两亭看，真是美景如画，尽展眼帘，既可俯瞰补园，又可借中部园景，这才领略到亭用"宜两"二字原因所在。

拙政园建于明嘉靖年间，为御史王献臣所建。"拙政"二字是取古书上"拙者之为政"的意思，表示园主不得志于朝，筑园以明志。几经易主，到了清太平天国战争后，这园的西部

Green Willows Bring the Spring into Two Gardens
—Zhuozheng Garden

"The bright moon shines deep into night; green willows bring the spring into two gardens."

Zhuozheng Garden, as it stands today, falls into two parts: the central part and the western part. Beyond the courtyard in the western part of Buyan Garden, pavilions and towers emerge here and there above the openwork walls. If you climb up Yiliang Pavilion, which is on top of the artificial mountain overlooking the garden, and gaze into the distance, lyrical and picturespue scenes will meet your eye. This tower borrows the scenery from the central part of the garden. It is not until now can one understand why the Tower got its name as Yiliang, meaning "appropriate for both parts".

Zhuozheng Garden was constructed during the reign of Emperor Jiajing in the Ming Dynasty by Wang Xianchen, an imperial censor, who had quit his position in court and returned to his hometown. The name Zhuozheng meaning "humble administrator", is taken from classics to express his idea of withdrawal: "Growing trees around the house, living a carefree and contented life, and watering vegetables in the garden for us to eat every day... it is a life that a humble administraor should live." The ownership of the garden changed several times until after the Taiping Rebellion of the Qing Dynasty when the garden was separated and the western part named Buyuan Garden. The two gardens borrow the scenery from each other so much so that they appear to be one garden though apart. A new garden east of the gardens acts as an expansion, following the acquisition of another garden called Guitianyuanju.

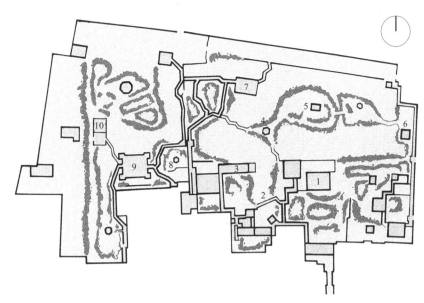

拙政园
| Zhuozheng Garden

1. 远香堂 | Yuanxiang Hall
2. 小飞虹 | Xiaofeihong
3. 香洲 | Xiangzhou
4. 荷风四面亭 | Hefengsimian Pavilion
5. 雪香云蔚亭 | Xuexiangyunwei Pavilion
6. 梧竹幽居 | Wuzhuyouju
7. 见山楼 | Jianshan Tower
8. 宜两亭 | Yiliang Pavilion
9. 三十六鸳鸯馆 | Sanshiliu Yuanyang Hall
10. 留听阁 | Liuting Belvedere

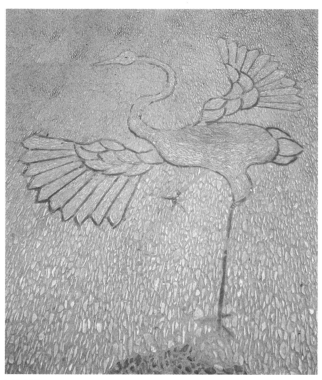

园中铺地
| The paving in the garden

分割了出去，名为"补园"。两园之景互相邻借，虽分犹合。如今东部新辟的园林则又是将另一园——"归田园居"合并过来的。

园以水为主，利用原来低洼之地巧妙安排：高者为山；低者拓池；利用其狭长水面，弯环曲岸；深处出岛，浅水藏矶，使水面饶弥漫之意。而亭台间出，桥梁浮波，以虚实之倒影与高低之层次构成了以水成景的画面。它是舒展成图，径缘池转，廊引人随，使游者入其园，信步观景，移步移影，此景以动观为主。偶尔暂驻之亭与可留之馆，予人以小休眺景，是以静观为辅也。

拙政园美在空灵，予人开朗之感，开朗中又具曲笔，所谓"园中有园"。故枇杷园、海棠春坞等小园幽静宜人，而于花墙窗棂中招大园之景于内，互呈其美者，苏州诸园以此为第一。故游人入是园，多少会产生闲云野鹤、

The original low-lying land is designed to be filled with water which plays an important role in this garden. Rockeries are built on the highland to emphasize the height and ponds are dug in the low-lying land to increase the depth. Along the long narrow waterway, curving embankments are built where the water turns; small islets are constructed where the water is deep; and rocks are laid under water where it is shallow, giving an impression of their reflections spreading on the water. Pavilions appearing above the water and bridges seemingly floating on waves form a view of water with layered real and imaginary reflections. As this illusory view unfolds, visitors are led along a winding path past a pond and through covered walkways. While strolling in the garden, visitors may see different views at every step they take. Most of the views may be better appreciated in an in-motion manner when visitors linger around without a stop. But occasionally, they may pause and take relaxations in a pavilion to enjoy the scenery afar in an in-position manner when sitting still.

The breathtaking beauty of Zhuozheng Garden lies in its ethereal quality that conveys a sense of openness; but quietly embedded in that openness is a labyrinth of scenic features, hence the so-called "garden inside garden". In small, tranquil gardens such as Pipa Garden and Haitangchunwu, the scenery of the larger garden is invited in through the lattices of the openwork walls. As a result, the borrowed scenery adds to the beauty of both the small garden and the large one. Among all the gardens in Suzhou, borrowing the scenery is best demonstrated here. A visitor who lingers along in this garden may be caught by a fantasy of being in the leisurely and carefree state of a cloud floating aimlessly in the sky or

拙政园中部湖景
| A Lake view in the central part of Zhuozheng Garden

静对湖山
| The lake and hills in tranquility

拙政园景观空阔，极富江南山林田园野趣，在苏州各园中较为独特。
Zhuozheng Garden enjoys a broad view of the scenery full of wild funs in
woods and fields in China south of Changjiang River, which is unique among
gardens in Suzhou.

去来无踪的雅致。春水之腻，夏水之浓，秋水之静，冬水之寒，与四时花木、朝夕光影构成了不同季节、不同时间的风光。

拙政园内有几处景点是绝不可错过的。远香堂是座四面敞开的荷花厅，荷香香远益清，所以称"远香堂"。人至此环身顾盼，一园之景可约略得之。前有山，后有岛，左有亭，右有台，而廊榭周接，木映花承，鸟飞于天，鱼跃于渊，景物之恬适，如饮香醇，此为主景。右转枇杷园，回首远眺，月门中逗入远处雪香云蔚亭，此为对景。经海棠春坞，循栏至梧竹幽居，一亭四出辟拱，人坐其中，四顾皆景矣。渡曲桥，登两岛，俯身临池，如入濠濮。望隔岸远香堂、香洲一带，华堂、船舫，皆出水面，风荷数柄，摇曳碧波之间，涟漪乍绉，泃足醒人。至西北角，缓步随石径登楼，一园之景毕于楼下，以"见山"二字名楼。

a wild crane wandering merrily by the water. One is impressed by the panorama of the four seasons when the water becomes colorful in the spring, steamy in the summer, tranquil in the autumn and chilly in the winter and the trees and flowers are bathed in the morning shades and the evening shadows.

There are several scenes in Zhuozheng Garden that a visitor cannot afford to miss. Yuanxiang Hall is an open-sided hall surrounded by lotus flowers. Yuanxiang means "fragrance reaching far into the distance" because of the sweet fragrance of the lotus flowers. From Yuanxiang Hall one can catch glimpses of a variety of scenes in the garden: a rockery in the front, an islet in the back, a pavilion on the left and a gazebo on the right. Here trees cast their shadows on the flowers, birds fly in an azure sky and fish jump in the pool. The peacefulness of this scene is as enjoyable to the senses as taking a sip of an aromatic wine. If one turns right and enters Pipa Garden, he can catch sight of Xuexiangyunwei Pavilion in the distance by looking back through an arched door. The pavilion in the arched door creates what is known as a Paired Scene. Go across Haitangchunwu and enter Wuzhuyouju where a pavilion is erected with arched doors on its four sides. When one pauses for a rest in the pavilion, he will find him self surrounded by beautifull scenery. Follow a zigzag brideg and you will step onto two connecting islets where when you lean over to look down into the pool, you fall into a dreamy, pleasurable state. In the distance across the pool, the magnificent Yuanxiang Hall and the boat-like Xiangzhou appear above the water with lotus leaves dancing in the wind above the gentle rippling wavelets, all which forms a truly inspiring scene. A leisurely walk along a footpath from the

香洲
| Xiangzhou

仿画舫之作，分前、中、后三舱。三舱高低错落，结构活泼。
It is an imitation of Huafang (Pleasure Boat) and has three cabins of Front Cabin, Middle Cabin and Rear Cabin. The three cabins which rise at verying heights display their vivideness in the structure.

空廊寥寂
| Solitude in an empty covered walkway

小飞虹

| Xiaofeihong

廊桥微拱，轻若飞虹。后有荷风四面亭、见山楼诸景。

The covered walkway is slightly arched like a flying rainbow. In the
background are Hefengsimian Pavilion and Jianshan Tower.

通过"别有洞天"的深幽园门进入园的西部，三十六鸳鸯馆居其中，南北二厅分居前后。南向观山景，北向看荷花，鸳鸯戏水，出没芙蕖间。隔岸浮翠阁出小山之上。所谓"浮翠"，是水绿、山碧、天青的意思。其旁濒池留听阁，取唐李商隐"留得残荷听雨声"之意，此处宜秋，故构此景。浮翠阁之东，倒影楼与宜两亭互为对景，而一水盈盈，高下相见，游人至此，一园之胜毕矣。迟迟举步，回首依恋，园尽而兴未阑也。

northwest corner of the Residence leads to a tower from which you can get a panoramic view of the garden. Because of this unique vantage point, the tower is named Jianshan, which means to have hills in sight.

The secluded gate of Bieyoudongtian leads into the western part of Zhuozheng Garden. In the center of this part lies Sanshiliu Yuanyang Hall; its south hall in the front faces a small mountain and its north hall in the back greets lotus flowers, a favorite habitat for colorful mandarin ducks. Above a small hill on the shore opposite the pavilion is Fucui Belvedere; Fucui indicates the clear water, green hills and blue sky. Next to this pavilion by the pool stands Liuting Belvedere which means keeping something to hear the sound. The name Liuting was taken from a poem by Li Shangyin, a famous poet of the Tang Dynasty. In the poem he says that the withered lotuses are kept for the poet to listen to the rain as it falls. The scenery is designed especially for autumn the best season to fully present it. To the east of Fucui Belvedere, Daoying Tower and Yiliang Pavilion form a paired scene with a body of water in between and with one standing high above the other.

It is here that the tour of Zhuozheng Garden comes to its end; and it is here that the visitor will have viewed all the scenery whose vibrant beauty renders the tour truly unforgettable and makes him reluctant to say good bye to the garden.

三十六鸳鸯馆内彩色玻璃窗
| Stained glass windows in Sanshiliu Yuanyang Hall

见山楼
| Jianshan Tower

小有亭台亦耐看

网师园

小有亭台亦耐看，并不容易做到，从艺术角度来讲，就是要以少胜多，要含蓄，要有不尽之意，要能得体，无过无不及，恰到好处。试以苏州网师园来谈谈，它是造园家推誉的小园典范。

网师园初建于宋代，原为南宋史正志的万卷堂故址，清乾隆年间（1736—1795）重建，同治年间（1862—1874）又重修，形成了今天的规模。园占地不广，但是人处其境，会感到称心悦目，宛转多姿，可坐可留，足堪盘桓竟夕，确实有其迷人之处，能

A Small Garden with Pavilions Is of Lasting Interest
—Wangshi Garden

It is not easy for a small garden with pavilions to be of lasting interest unless it possesses memorable features such as those found in Wangshi Garden in Suzhou. This garden is implicit in expression and infinite in meaning, a good illustration of the aesthetic appeal that less is more. Being highly commended by experts, this garden is classically representative of small gardens.

First constructed in the Song Dynasty, Wangshi Garden was originally the site for Wanjuan Hall of Mr. Shi Zhengzhi, a high-ranking official in the Southern Song Dynasty. It expanded to its present size after being rebuilt during the Qianlong reign (1736-1795) and renovated again during the Tongzhi reign (1862-1874). Despite its miniature size, the garden's compact layout and changeable scenes are so attractive to a visitor that he feels absorbed by its vibrant beauty. Its alluring charm can always be appropriately reflected no matter whether it is described with plain language or stated in simple words.

Chinese gardens, which are usually integrated with a dwelling area, form a part of official residences. Influenced by the patriarchal ideology of the feudal society, traditional Chinese residences follow rigid design patterns, whereas the gardens present natural landscapes fashioned after famous mountains and rivers, which bring flavor and add color to life. The gardens and dwelling areas in Wangshi Garden are both well known for their exquisiteness albeit their small size. The main residence includes only a living room for meeting visitors and holding banquets, and a couple of

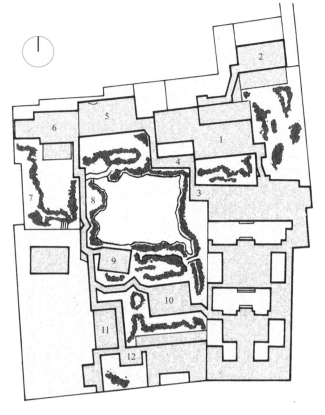

网师园
| Wangshi Garden

1. 五峰书屋 | Wufeng Study
2. 梯云室 | Tiyun Chamber
3. 射鸭廊 | Sheya Corridor
4. 竹外一枝轩 | Zhuwaiyizhi Gallery
5. 看松读画轩 | Kansongduhua Gallery
6. 殿春簃 | Dianchun Pavilion
7. 冷泉亭 | Lengquan Pavilion
8. 月到风来亭 | Yuedaofenglai Pavilion
9. 濯缨水阁 | Zhuoying Waterside Pavilion
10. 小山丛桂轩 | Xiaoshanconggui Gallery
11. 蹈和馆 | Daohe Pavilion
12. 琴室 | Qinshi Pavilion

网师园月到风来亭
| Yuedaofenglai Pavilion in Wangshi Garden

达到"淡语皆有味，浅语皆有致"的艺术境界。

中国园林往往与住宅相连，是住宅建筑的组成部分。中国传统住宅多受封建社会的宗法思想影响，布局较为严谨，而园林部分却多范山模水，以自然景色出现，可调剂生活，增进舒适的情味。网师园的园林和住宅都不算大，皆以精巧见称，主宅亦只有会客饮宴用的大厅和起居的内厅。主宅旁则以楼屋为过渡，与西部的园林形成若接若分的处理，手法巧妙。

从轿厅西首入园，可看到门上刻有"网师小筑"四字。"网师"是托丁"渔隐"的意思，因此，园的中心是一个大池。进园，有曲廊接四面厅，厅名"小山丛桂轩"。轩前隔以花墙，山幽桂馥，香藏不散。轩东有便道，可直贯南北。径莫妙于曲，莫便于直，因为是"便道"，所以是用直道，供当时仆人作传达、递送之用。蹈和馆、琴室位轩西，小院回廊，迂回曲折。"欲扬先抑"，"未歌先敛"，此处造园

sleeping rooms. Next to the main residence stands a storied house which builds a connection with the gardens in the west.

Upon entering Wangshi Garden from the west of Sedan Hall, one may see over the gate an inscription of four Chinese characters: *Wang Shi Xiao Zhu* with Wang Shi meaning fishermen's hermitage. This explains the existence of a large pond in the center of the garden. Inside the garden lie zigzag covered walkways leading to a four-sided open hall called Xiaoshanconggui Gallery. The front of the hall is fenced off by a tracery wall behind which osmanthus sends off a densely sweet scent in the small mountains.

To the east of the hall, a pathway extends from south to north right through the garden. Although a winding pathway is more interesting, a straight one is more convenient for it provided a speedy way for servants to deliver messages. To the west of the pavilion stand Daohe Pavilion and Qinshi Pavilion, where zigzag covered walkways wind through them. The gardening technique of suppression prior to emancipation is featured here. North of Xiaoshanconggui Gallery is walled with rockeries made of the Yellow Stones, thus called Yungang. When going along the covered walkways and crossing over the bumpiness, one may stop and relax in a pavilion named Yuedaofenglai, and enjoy a broad view of the pond with its mirror-like waves, steep fishing rocks, and meandering colorful bridges. Cloud images change with the movement of the water, resulting in an alternation of illusion and reality near and afar. The name of the pavilion is to depict the enchanting scenery. "With trickling water encroaching upon stairs, I dig a pool to invite the moon; meticulously painted buildings waving in water, lotus flowers

名园依绿水
| Clear water brings life to a garden

月到风来亭和濯缨水阁

| Yuedaofenglai Pavilion and Zhuoying Waterside Pavilion

也用此技法，故小山丛桂轩的北面用黄石山围隔，称"云岗"。随廊越陂，有亭可留，名"月到风来亭"。视野开阔，明波若镜，渔矶高下，画桥迤逦，俱呈一池之中，其间高下虚实，云水变幻，骋怀游目，咫尺千里。"涓涓流水细浸阶，凿个池儿，招个月儿来，画栋频摇动，芙蕖尽倒开。"亭名"月到风来"正写此妙镜。云岗以西，小阁临流，名"濯缨"，与看松读画轩隔水相呼。轩是园的主厅，其前古木若虬，老根盘结于苔石间，仿佛一幅画面。轩旁有廊一曲，与竹外一枝轩接连，东廊名"射鸭"，是一半亭，与池西之月到风来亭相映，凭栏得静观之趣。俯视池水，弥漫无尽，聚而支分，去来无踪，盖得力于溪口、湾头、石矶的巧妙安排，以假象逗人。桥与步石环池而筑，其用意在不分割水面，看去增加支流深远之意。至于驳岸有级，出水流矶，增人浮水之感。而亭、台、廊、榭无不面水，使全园处处有水可依。园不在大，泉不在广。唐杜

in full blossom are flickeringin the wind." West of Yungang is Zhuoying, a pavilion which stands near the water and which loosely corresponds to Kansongduhua Gallery. In front of this gallery, which serves as the main studio in the garden, old dragon-like cypress trees, coiling and tangling their roots amidst mossy rocks, look like real-life paintings. Next to the gallery is a zigzag covered walkway, that leads to Zhuwaiyizhi Gallery. The eastern part of the covered walkway known as Sheya, is a half pavilion corresponding to Yuedaofenglai Pavilion in the western part of the pond. One may get an excellent view of this pavilion by leaning upon balustrades in the eastern covered walkway. The pavilion overlooks a pond which gives the illusion of a vast infiniteness. This fascinating effect is attributed to the ingenious arrangement of stream ends, docks and rocks, whose artificial appearances look whimsical. Bridges and footpaths are built around the pond with the intent not to break the view of the water surface, but to intensify the vastness of the water. Stairs are laid out along the banks and water flows from rocks, generating an illusion of people floating on water. Pavilions, walkways and towers are all placed near the water, creating an effect that there is always water for each scenic spot to lean on in the garden. A garden distinguishes itself not because it is big; in the same vein, a spring is famous not because it spreads afar. This garden is well illustrated by a line from a poem by poet Du Fu in Tang Dynasty: "clear water brings life to a garden". Inspired by Bailian Pool at Tiger Hill, the elegant simplicity of the plain rocks around the pond creates a profound atmosphere.

In the western part of the garden is Dianchun Pavilion, originally a greenhouse for planting Chinese herbaceous peonies. The pavilion is

看松读画轩
| Kansongduhua Gallery
此轩为园中画室。轩前遍植松柏佳木，景致清幽。
This gallery is a painting studio in the garden. Pine and cypress trees
are planted in front of the gallery, creating a mood of traquility and
peacefulness.

甫诗所谓"名园依绿水",正好为此园写照。池周山石,看去平易近人,蕴藉多姿,它的蓝本出自虎丘白莲池。

　　网师园西部殿春簃本来是栽植芍药花的,因为一春花事,芍药开在最后,所以名为"殿春"。小轩三间,复带书房,竹、石、梅、蕉隐于窗后,每当微阳淡淡地照着时,宛如一幅浅色的图画。苏州的园林,此园的构思最佳。因为园小,建筑物处处凌虚,空间扩大,"透"字的妙用,随处得之。轩前面东为假山,与其西曲廊相对。西南的角上有一小水池,名为"涵碧",清澈醒人,与中部大池有脉可通,存"水贵有源"之意。泉上筑亭,名"冷泉",南面略置峰石,为殿春簃的对景。余地用卵石平整铺地。它与中部水池同一原则,都是以大片面积,形成水陆的对比。前者以石点水,后者以水点石。在总体上,利用建筑与山石的对比,相互更换,使人看去觉得变化多端。

named Dianchun, meaning late spring, for Chinese herbaceous peonies don't come into full bloom until late spring in contrast to other flowers that are in full blossom in spring. The pavilion consists of three partitions with a study where bamboos, rocks, plum trees and plantains are hidden behind windows, giving rise to an impression of paintings bathed in pale sunshine. The design of this garden surpasses that of all other gardens in Suzhou. Because the garden is small, buildings are ereted overhead to make the space seem much larger than it is. This intriguing application of "seeing-through" is revealed in details everwhere. For example, east of the pavilion is a rockery opposite zigzag covered walkways in the west. In the southeast lies the small, clear Hanbi Pool, which is connected to the large pond in the center of the garden, implying the source of the spring. A pavilion called Lengquan is above the spring. On its southern side are large steep rocks sparsely placed to form paired scenes with Dianchun Pavilion. The ground is covered with pebbles. The layout of this part follows the same garden design principle for the design of the pond in the center of the garden that is, to form a sharp contrast between water and land. The former design decorates water with rocks, while the latter one decorates rocks with water. On the whole, variable contrasts between buildings and rocks are used to present changing scenes to visitors.

　　It is difficult to make a large garden of a million *mu* compact, while it is equally hard to render a small garden of several *mu* as spacious. In a large but compact garden one does not feel tired when touring in it; in a small but spacious garden one feels as if there remains a lot to be seen. So when viewed in an in-position manner, i.e. at a standstill or in an in-motion manner, i.e.

殿春簃内窗景
| Views through windows inside Dianchun Pavilion

万顷之园难在紧凑，数亩之园难在宽绰。紧凑则不觉其大，游无倦意，宽绰则不觉局促，览之有物，故以静、动观园，有缩地扩基之妙，而奴役风月，左右游人，极尽构思之巧。网师园无旱船[1]、大桥，建筑物尺度略小，数量适可而止，停停当当，像个小园格局，这在造园学上称为"得体"。

至于树木栽植，小园宜多落叶，以疏植之，取其空透，此为以疏救塞，因为园小往往务多的缘故。小园布景有中空而边实，有中实而边空，前者如网师园，后者环秀山庄略似之。总之，在有限面积要有较大空间，这些空间要有变化，所以利用建筑、花墙、山石等分隔，以形成多种层次，而曲水弯环，又在布局上多不尽之意。造园之妙，盖在于此。

注释：

1. 旱船是中国园林常见的一种建筑形式，为水边建造的船形建筑物，以供临水游想、眺望。

when wandering along, a garden may seem to be shrunken or enlarged. With this ingenious arrangement, the moon and wind are seemingly controlled and visitors are enchanted. Without land boats[1] and big bridges in Wangshi Garden, buildings are constructed relatively small in size and in number, in a way that a small garden is supposed to be. This is exactly what we mean by "appropiate" in garden design.

As for the selection of plants, deciduous trees should be planted sparsely in a smallgarden to create a sense of openness. The intent is to spare the garden from looking being cramped by keeping objects sparse in number, since there are often too many objects in a small garden. The scenery in a small garden should be arranged in a pattern. That is sparse in the middle but dense on the edges, or being dense in the middle but sparse on the edges. Wangshi Garden is a fine example of the former pattern, and Huanxiu Mountain Resort illustrates the latter pattern. In general, to make a small area look spacious, one must have variety in the space; therefore, buildings, tracery walls and rocks should be well juxtaposed to create multi-dimensions. In addition, the layout of a garden, the meandering water and the curving banks should be used to impart a sense of infinity. The mystery of garden design probably lies in this.

Notes:

1. A land boat is a boat-like building built by waterside for visitors to relax and admire the scenery in the distance. It is a structure commonly used in Chinese garden design.

网师小景 | A view of plants in Wangshi Garden

曲廊 | Zigzag covered walkways

庭院深深深几许

留园

"小廊回合曲阑斜"，"庭院深深深几许"，这些唐宋人的词句描绘了中国庭院建筑之美。

苏州留园与拙政园一样，皆初建于明代，亦同样经过后人重修，其中部假山出自明代叠山匠师周秉忠之手。留园又名"寒碧山庄"，因为清刘蓉峰[1]重整此园时，多植白皮松，使园更显清俊，故以"寒碧"二字名之。刘氏好石，列十二峰宠其园，如冠云一峰，即驰誉至今。

进入留园，那狭长的进口时暗时明，几经转折，始现花墙当面，仅见漏窗中隐现池石，及转身至明瑟楼，方见水石横陈，花木环覆，不觉此身已置画中矣。恰似白居易"千呼万唤始出来，犹抱琵琶半遮面"之诗意。

A Deep Garden Stretches into Infinity

—Liuyuan Garden

"Railings wind along walkways" and "A deep garden may reach profoundly far" are lines from the Ci-Poetry in the Tang and Song Dynasties, describing the architectural beauty of Chinese gardens.

Liuyuan Garden, just like Zhuozheng Garden in Suzhou, was first built in the Ming Dynasty And has been reconstructed throughout generations. The rockeries in the center are the works of Zhou Bingzhong, a famous rockery expert in the Ming Dynasty. This garden is also known as Hanbi Mountain Resort following the reconstruction by Liu Rongfeng[1] in the Qing Dynasty. During the reconstruction, a number of lacebark pines were planted to bring a sense of cool beauty to the garden. Hence the garden was also know as Hanbi, meaning cool and beautiful. Twelve rock peaks were erected in the garden as a result of Liu's intense love of rockery. One, Guanyun Peak, for instance, has remained well known since then.

Upon entering the garden, a long and narrow passge leads a visitor through a few turns, some bright and others dark, to a tracery wall through which he may faintly detect rocks in a pool. It is not until he turns around and reaches Mingse Tower that he can see rocks submerged in the water and trees and flowers trailing all around. And then he realizes that he has unconsciously become a part of a poetic painting in the manner depicted in the famous lines by Bai Juyi: "The beauty showed up after being invited a thousand times, still hiding half her face behind her *pipa* lute."

In the central part of the garden, waters are embraced by rockeries. Quxi Tower with its white-washed walls and beautiful lattice windows is situated in the east, its reflection floating on the water. Keting Pavilion peches on the top of the North Hill; opposite Quxi Tower stands Wenmuxixiang Gallery, hidden behind rocks and seemingly reluctant to show itself. Sightseeing covered walkways, snaking up and down and around the garden, end at the southern end of the pool. The Hanbi Mountain Chamber is a hall

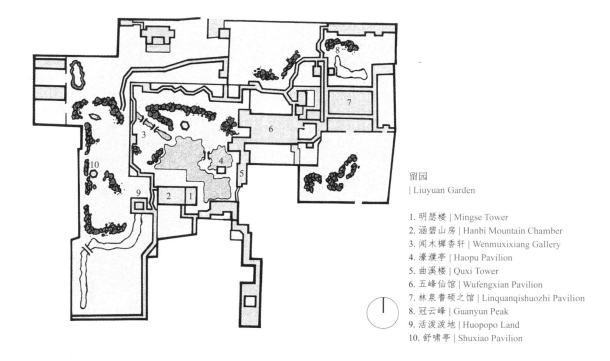

留园
| Liuyuan Garden

1. 明瑟楼 | Mingse Tower
2. 涵碧山房 | Hanbi Mountain Chamber
3. 闻木樨香轩 | Wenmuxixiang Gallery
4. 濠濮亭 | Haopu Pavilion
5. 曲溪楼 | Quxi Tower
6. 五峰仙馆 | Wufengxian Pavilion
7. 林泉耆硕之馆 | Linquanqishuozhi Pavilion
8. 冠云峰 | Guanyun Peak
9. 活泼泼地 | Huopopo Land
10. 舒啸亭 | Shuxiao Pavilion

留园明瑟楼及绿荫
| Mingse Tower and Lüyin in Liuyuan Garden

此园之中部有山环水，曲溪楼居其东，粉墙花槛，倒影历历。可亭踞北山之巅。闻木樨香轩与曲溪楼相对，但又隐于石间，藏而不露。游廊环园，起伏高低，止于池南。涵碧山房，荷花厅也，其西北小桥，架三层，各因地势形成立体交通。临水跨谷，各具功能，又各饶情趣，于数丈之地得之，巧于安排也。翘首西望，远眺枫林若醉，倾入池中，红泛碧波，引人遐想，得借景之妙。

园之东部多院落，楼堂错落，廊庑回缭，峰石水池，间列其前，游人至此，莫知所至。揖峰轩、五峰仙馆、林泉耆硕之馆、冠云楼等参差组合，各自成区，而又互通消息，实中寓虚，其运用墙之分隔、窗之空透，使变化多端。而风清月朗，花影栏杆，良宵更为宜人。

中部之水，东部之屋，西部之山，各有主体，各具特征，而皆有节奏韵律，人能得之者变化而已。而"园必隔，水必曲"之理，于此园最能体现。

注释：

1. 刘蓉峰，清嘉庆年间（1796—1820）园林学家，为苏州留园的重要修整人之一。

surrounded by lotus flowers. The bridges to its northwest form a three-decker passage following the natural terrain on the site. These buildings, either built by water or over valleys complement different tastes and add distinctive functions to the garden. All this is achieved on a land of dozens of feet, which demonstrates an ingenious design. When a visitor looks to the west, he sees a beautiful view of maple trees extending all the way down to the pool where the drunken red maple leaves mingle with the blue waves, leaving him spellbound. This is an excellent example of borrowing the scenery.

There are a number of courtyards in the eastern part of the garden where storied-towers and halls are uniquely arranged in a deliberate disorder with zigzag covered walkways, rocks, and pools scattered in the front. Enchanted by the impressive scene, a visitor nevertheless feels bewildered about where he is. Yifeng Gallery, Wufengxian Pavilion, Linquanqishuozhi Pavilion and Guanyun Tower are arranged at different levels of height so that they look independent from one another on the one hand, but communicate with one another on the other hand, a realization of reality based upon fantasy. Walls are used to separate these buildings which are then linked by perforated windows, thus resulting in a variety of scenes during day time. The night time is even more dramatic with the shadows of flowers swaying in a gentle breeze along the covered walkways in clear moonlight.

In the garden, the waters in the central part, the buildings in the eastern part and the rockeries in the western part all convey distinctive themes, features and rhythms of their own. To achieve this effect, the arrangement of scenes in a garden must be made full of change. Liuyuan Garden is the best illustration of the principle that "a garden must be separated into parts, and the water in a garden must be meandering."

Notes:

1. Liu Rongfeng, a garden designer during the reign of Emperor Jiaqing (1796-1820) of the Qing Dynasty, was one of the leading people responsible for the reconstruction of Liuyuan Garden in Suzhou.

冠云峰
| Guanyun Peak

留园冠云峰传为北宋花石纲遗物，高约 9 米，具"瘦、皱、透、漏"
之妙，为苏州园林所仅见。
Guanyun Peak in Liuyuan Garden is rumored to be the relic of the stones
known as Huashigang in the Northern Song Dynasty. About nine meters
in heiht, its unique features of being slim, wrinkled, transparent and
perforate make it the only one in gardens of Suzhou.

庭院深深
| A deep garden

留园入口处，以回廊曲院、洞门漏窗来增加空间层次，别具匠心。
The entrance of Liuyuan Garden demonstrates the ingenuity of a garden design master. Here zigzag covered walkways, curved coutyards, arched doors and perforated windows are employed to enlarge the space at various heights.

林泉耆硕之馆内景

| An inside view of Liquanqishuozhi Pavilion

园东林泉耆硕之馆为一鸳鸯厅式的厅堂，北面可赏冠云峰之景。室
内的圆光罩为厅堂的分隔。

Linquanqishuozhi Pavilion in the eastern part of the garden, is a hall
presented in a paired style where one may admire the scenery of
Guanyun Peak on its northern side. The circular door serves as a room-
divider.

留园濠濮亭
| Haopu Pavilion in Liuyuan Garden
其为中部园景，后为曲溪楼。
Haopu Pavilion is a scenic spot in the central part, behind which stands
Quxi Tower.

幽谷清溪假亦真

环秀山庄

真山如假方奇，假山似真始妙——这样的真山、假山才能看，能游，能想，能居。这是美境，亦是造园叠山所难能求得的。中国园林假山自有佳构，而现存者当推苏州环秀山庄为第一。

环秀山庄原来布局：前堂名"有谷"，南向前后点石，翼以两廊及对照轩。堂后筑环秀山庄，面对山林，水萦如带。一亭浮波，一亭枕山。两贯长廊，尽处有楼。循山径登楼，可俯观全园，飞雪泉在其下，补秋舫则横卧北端。

主山位于园之东部，浮水一亭在池之西北隅，因面对飞雪泉故名"问

Artificial Deep Valleys and Clear Streams Become Real

—Huanxiu Mountain Resort

Real mountains appear artificial while artificial rockeries look rael. Such real mountains and artificial rockeries are worth visiting, admiring, and meditating on and living by, This effect is very difficult to achieve with a pile of rocks. There are the ingenious designs we come to expect in a classical Chinese garden. Huanxiu Mountain Resort in Suzhou ranks number one among such rockeries.

In the layout of Huanxiu Mountain Resort, the front hall is named Yougu, south of which rocks are scattered. Covered walkways and chambers are set up on both sides of the hall. Behind the hall lies Huanxiu Mountain Resort, which, encircled by limpid water, overlooks the woods. One pavilion is floating above water and the other is perched on a mountain. At the end of two long covered walkways stands a tower. When a visitor climbs up to the tower by following a footpath in the mountain, he has a panoramic view of the resort, where Feixue Spring sits at the foot of the mountain and Buqiu Boat lies to its north.

The main mountain lies in the eastern part of the Mountain Rseort. The pavilion floating above water in the northwest corner of the pool is named Wenquan (Asking Spring) for it stands opposite Feixue Spring. A walk from the southwest of the pavilion, across Sanqu Bridge, along a precipitous footpath and into a valley leads to a cave that lies to the northwest of the resort, and winds through the valley. Inside the cave, daylight shines faintly through a few scattered skylights and stalactites hang down here and there. Following stone steps, going up a rocky mountain and across a rock beam, one steps into a deep and horrendous valley where light is dim in the gloomy and thick air. Here a bridge can be seen overhead, looking as if it is

环秀山庄小桥流水
| The bridge and running water in Huanxiu Mountain Resort

泉"。自亭西南渡三曲桥，入崖道，弯入谷中。有洞自西北来，横贯崖谷，经石洞，天窗隐约，钟乳垂垂，踏步石，上蹬道，渡石梁，幽谷森严，阴翳蔽日。而一桥横跨，欲飞还敛。飞雪泉在望，隐然若屏。沿山巅，达主峰，穿石洞，过飞桥，至于山后，枕山一亭，名"半潭秋水一房山"。沿泉而出，山蹊渐低，峰石参差，补秋舫在焉。东西两门额曰"凝青""摇碧"，足以概括全园景色。其西为飞雪泉石壁，洞有飞石，极险巧。

园初视之，山重水复，身入其境，移步换影，变化多端。"溪水因山成曲折，山蹊随地作低平"，得真山水之妙谛，却以极简洁洗练手法出之。山中空而雄浑，谷曲折而幽深。山中藏洞屋，内贯涧流，佐以步石、崖道，仿佛天然。澄道自东北来，与涧流相会于步石，至此，仰则青天一线，俯则清流几曲，几疑身在万山中。上层

halfway soaring into the sky, but is held back. The faintly visible Feixue Spring now appears like a screen. Climbing over the mountain-top leads one to the main peak, then through the cave and across the flying bridge until he arrives at the rear of the mountain where within sight is a pavilion named as Bantanqiushui Yifangshan. When leaving the spring, a visitor finds a footpath gradually going down among scattered rocks to the bottom of the mountain where Buqiu Boat lies. The signs on the east and west gate towers read Ningqing and Yaobi to highlight the scenery in the resort. West of the signs stands the stone wall of Feixue Spring, by which is a ravine where there are stones that appear to be flying, displaying expuisite perilousness.

At first sight, a visitor sees mountain ranges and a vast expanse of water in the garden. When he walks further into the garden, he witnesses varying scenes with every step he takes. "A stream meanders around the mountain; a mountain footpath blends in with the terrain." The essence of mountains and waters described in poerty is materialized here in a simplistic and succinct way. The mountains are hollow yet appear vigorous and firm, and the valleys are winding yet appear deep and serene. Mountains harbor the cave with a narrow steam oozing through stone steps and precipitous footpaths render the scenery more natural. The rocky mountain path from the northeast meets a narrow stream at the stone steps, where with a slit of sky above and a limpid stream of water below a visitor is lost in a fantasy of being in the midst of thousands of mountains. The upper passage ring, crossed over by a flying beam, streches out over streams and valleys, forming tour routes through a myriad of multi-layered peaks and valleys where a visitor soon loses his sense of directon. The Mountain Resort covers an area of about 1600 spuare kilometers with 333 square

由补秋舫望假山
| A view of the rockery from Buqiu Boat

环道，跨以飞梁，越溪度谷，组成重层游览线，千岩万壑，方位莫测。园占地约 1600 平方米，而假山占地约 333 平方米，小巧精致，实难以置信。

山以深幽取胜，水以弯环见长，无一笔不曲，无一处不藏，设想布景，层出新意。水有源，山有脉，息息相通。以有限面积，造无限空间。亭廊皆出山脚，补秋舫若浮水洞之上，因地处出麓也。西北角飞雪岩，视主山为小，水口、飞石，妙胜画本。旁建小楼，有檐瀑，下临清潭，仿佛曲尽而余味绕梁间。而亭前一泓，宛若点睛。

移天缩地，为造园家之惯技，而因地制宜，就地取材，择景模拟，造石成山，则因人而别，各抒其长。

环秀山庄之假山是清代乾隆年间叠山名家戈裕良[1]的作品，它的蓝本是苏州大石山。正如他另一作品——常熟燕园模自虞山一样，法同式异，各具地方风格。

kilometers occupied by rockeries; truly this is an incredibly tiny and exquisitely designed garden.

Mountains excel in their serenity and stillness whereas a stream exults in its twists and turns. There is nowhere which is not curved and no scene not hidden. The layout of the garden showcases the creativity and ingenuity of the designer. Streams have their sources and mountains their veins, which keep them naturally connected. An infinite large space is created in a finite tiny area. Pavilions and coverd walkways are all set at the foot of mountains, and Buqiu Boat looks as if it is floating over a cave in water, since it is located at the foot of a mountain. Feixue Peak in the northwest corner is dwarfed by the main mountain; the stream ends and flying stones appear even more beguiling than those on a Chinese mountain-and-water painting. Nearby is a small tower with water rushing down from its eaves into a deep pool below, creating an effect similat to that when a music is over, its tune is still echoing in the air. The pool with translucent water in front of the pavilion is just like the finishing touches in a Chinese painting.

To borrow the scenery and to miniaturize garden scenes are the customary practices used by garden designers. However, they distinguish themselves by applying the specific skills they are good at in adapting their designs to natural features of a landscape, in taking advantage of local materials, in turning stones into rockeries, and in choosing natural scenery for imitation for their gardens.

The rockeries in Huanxiu Mountain Resort are outstanding works of Ge Yuliang[1], a well known rock-piling master during the reign of Emperor Qianlong in the Qing Dynasty. Just as Yanyuan Garden in Changshu, another work of his, which was built after Yushan Mountain, the rockery of Huanxiu Mountain Resort was an

幽谷清溪
| Deep valley and clear stream

环秀山庄叠石得真山水之韵，中有石室、飞梁、崖道，处理手法巧妙。
The rockeries in Huanxiu Mountain Resort capture the natural rhythms
of mountains and water. Stone houses, flying bridges and precipitous
footpaths in the cave are designed in a superb ingenious way.

戈裕良的叠山技艺成就卓越。他总结前人叠山技术，树立了体形大、腹中空，中构洞壑、洞谷的乾隆至嘉庆年间的假山风格，并首创造洞技巧中的"钩带法"，如造环洞桥。这种方法能使洞的顶壁一气，结构合理，能运用少量的石叠大型的山。而山石的皴法悉符画本，其意兼宋元画本之长，宛转多姿，浑若天成。叠山之妙法具备，其作品乃为中国假山艺术中之上品。

注释：

1. 戈裕良，清江苏常州著名园林叠山家。生于乾隆二十九年（1764），卒于道光十年（1830）。

imitation of Dashi Mountain in Suzhou. Both of his works, guided by the same principles, demonstrate different tactics and represent distinctive local features.

Ge Yuliang is famous for his outstanding achievements in building rockeries. Drawing on the expertise of his predecessors in the rock-piling art, he successfully created a unique rockery style during the reigns of Emperors Jiaqing and Qianlong in the Qing Dynasty. This style is characterized by the use of large hollow rocks and of streams winding through dark caves and deep valleys. The application of his original cave-building technique of interlocking stones, as in building a bridge ring around a cave, succeeds in connecting a roof and walls smoothly into a well-balanced structure; he was also noted for building large rockeries with a very small amount of rocks. The veins of rockeries stand out in the same way as they do in the fine paintings of the Song and Yuan Dynasties. The sheer artistry changes the man-made rockery to look completely natural. Because of the skillful compiling of all the rock piling technipues, the rockeries in this mountain resort are indeed the very best of Chinese rockeries.

Notes:

1. Ge Yuliang, born in the twenty-ninth year of the reign of Emperor Qianlong (1764) and died in the tenth year of the reign of Emperor Daoguang (1830) was a famous rockery master from Changzhou, Jiangsu Province in the Qing Dynasty.

问泉亭
| Wenquan Pavilion

二分明月在扬州

扬州园林

江苏扬州市西郊有瘦西湖，湖以"瘦"字命名，已点出其景致特色。

瘦西湖原是一条狭长水面，两岸以往全是私家园林，万柳拂水，楼阁掩映，瘦西湖正是游诸园的水上交通要道。清时，因乾隆南巡，加建了白塔与五亭桥，虽都是模仿北京北海的建筑，可是风格各有不同。从城内的小秦淮乘画舫缓缓入湖，登小金山俯瞰全湖，坐在"月观"，眺望"四桥烟雨"，空濛迷离，婉约如一首清歌。

瘦西湖的景妙在"巧"，最巧是从小金山下沿堤至"钓鱼台"。白塔与五亭桥分占圆拱门内，回视小金山，又在另一拱门中，所谓"面面有情"，

Clear Moonlight Is Tangible Only in Yangzhou
—Gardens in Yangzhou

In the western outskirts of Yangzhou, Jiangsu Province, lies Slender West Lake. As its name suggests, the word "slender" proclaims the main feature of the lake.

Slender West Lake used to be a narrow stretch of water along which were dotted private gardens. The delicate limbs of weeping willows trail through the water and towers and pavilions peak from behind walls. It is by this waterway that a visitor may access these gardens. In the Qing Dynasty, the White Pagoda and Wuting Bridge were established to welcome Emperor Qianlong during his trip to the south. Although these buildings are copied after the ones in Beihai Park in Beijing, each building nevertheless displays its own unique style. Usually a visitor starts his tour by taking the Huafang (Pleasure Boat) from the Little Qinhuai River inside the City of Yangzhou and rides slowly into the lake. He may then ascend Little Jinshan Rockery to get a panoramic view of the lake, and when he sits down for a rest in Yueguan Pavilion, he may become enchanted by the dreamlike scenery of Siqiaoyanyu in the distance.

The beauty of Slender West Lake lies in its ingenuity of design, which reaches its climax at Diaoyu Terrace. After descending Little Jinshan Rockery and idling along the lakeshore, a visitor arrives at Diaoyu Terrace where the White Pagoda and Wuting Bridge emerge into view through the round arched doors of the pavilion. What is more, when he looks back, he may see Little Jinshan Rockery through yet another round arched door of the pavilion. It is hard to fully understand the charming vistas that can be seen in every direction until one is actually there. Such fantastic views inside views can be found only at this vantage point. A boat trip is the best way to experience the mystical beauty of theis scenery where threads of

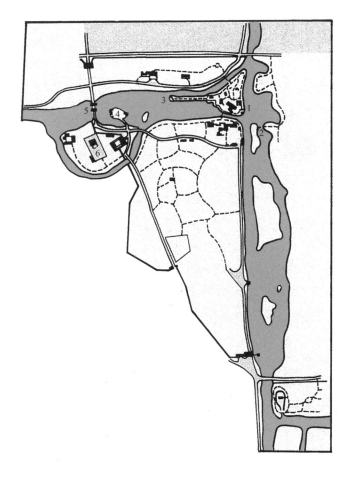

瘦西湖
| Slender West Lake

1. 小金山 | Little Jinshan Rockery
2. 四桥烟雨 | Siqiaoyanyu
3. 吹台 | Chuitai Terrace
4. 凫庄 | Fuzhuang Village
5. 五亭桥 | Wuting Bridge
6. 白塔 | The White Pagoda

五亭桥瘦西湖
| Wuting Bridge in Slender West Lake

于此方得。而雨丝风片，烟波画船，人影衣香，赤栏小桥，游览应以舟行最能体会到其中妙处。

平山堂是瘦西湖一带最高的据点。堂前可望江南山色，有一联："晓起凭阑，六代青山都在眼；晚来把酒，二分明月正当头。"将景物概括殆尽。此堂位置正与隔江之山齐平，故称"平山堂"。其他如"白塔晴云""春台明月""蜀冈晚照"等二十四景亦招徕了不少游人。如今，平山堂所在地的大明寺又建了唐高僧鉴真[1]纪念堂，修整了西园。西园有山中之湖，并有天下第五泉，饶山林泉石之趣。

扬州以名园胜，名园以叠石胜。扬州具有地方特色的四季假山能使游者从中领略到不同季节的风情。个园的假山就是其中代表作。

个园园门内满植修竹，竹间配置石笋，以一真一假的幻觉形成了春景。湖石山是夏山，山下池水流入洞谷，其洞如屋，曲折幽邃，山石形态多变

rain amid puffs of wind and the sound of the water lapping against the pleasure boats charm their passengers as they travel under little bridges with red railings.

The best vantage point of Slender West Lake is Pingshan Hall from which the finest scenery south of Changjiang River unfolds before the eyes. A couplet in the front of the hall reads, "Leaning on the railing at dawn, I feel surrounded by the green mountains of six dynasties; drinking alone at dark, I am bathed in the clear moonlight." The soothing beauty of the scenery is vividly captured in these lines. The hall is named Pingshan because it is at the same level (*ping*) as the mountain (*shan*) on the other side of the river. Other scenic spots which attract large numbers of visitors include Baitaqingyun, Chuntaimingyue and Shugangwanzhao among the well-known twenty-four scenes. In recent years a memorial hall in memory of Jianzhen[1], an eminent monk in the Tang Dynasty, was built in Daming Temple near Pingshan Hall. The Western Garden, which has also been reconstructed, includes a lake surrounded by mountains and Tianxia Diwu Spring. The garden's setting with the mountains, the woods, the rocks, and the spring is captivating!

Yangzhou excels in famous gardens which in turn excel in stunning rockeries. The rockeries of four seasons, rich in local features of Yangzhou, delight visitors with changing seasons, a masterpiece of which is the rockey in Geyuan Garden.

Geyuan Garden, emphasizing bamboos with grotesquely shaped rocks laid among them just inside the enterance fabricates an imaginary scene of spring. Lake stone rockery depicts a vision of summer with rocks of various sizes and interesting shapes and a stream threading its way through a deep and serene-looking cave at its foot in turn. This rockery provides an ideal place for one to retreat from the summer heat. Autumn is represented by a yellow stone rockey, which faces the west. At sunset, when the sinking

登小金山俯瞰瘦西湖
| A bird's-eye view of Slender West Lake from Little Jinshan Rockery
瘦西湖最美是在烟雨中，白塔、凫庄、五亭桥和垂岸杨柳若隐若现，
如画如诗。
Slender West Lake looks most beautiful in mist and rain when the White
Pagoda, Fuzhuang Village, Wuting Bridge and weeping willows along
embankments appear faintly discernible.

化，是夏日纳凉的好地方。秋山是一座黄石山，山的主面向西。夕阳西下，一抹红霞映照在山上，不但山势显露，并且色彩倍觉斑斓，而山的本身又拔地数丈，峻峭凌云，宛如一幅秋山图，是秋日登高的理想所在。山中还置小院、石桥、石室等，人在洞中上下盘旋，造奇致胜。登山顶北眺绿杨城郭，瘦西湖、平山堂诸景一一招入园内。山之南有石一丘，其色白，巧妙地象征"雪"意，是为冬景。从不同的欣赏角度，构不同季节的假山，唯扬州有之。

楼阁建筑是中国园林的重要组成部分，楼阁嵯峨，游廊高下，予人以极深刻之印象。而扬州园林除水石之胜外，其厅堂高敞，多置于一园的主要位置，作为宴客畅聚之用，这是因为园林的主人皆属富商，需要保持必要的交际活动。厅堂都为层楼，其联缀之游廊亦有两层，称"复道廊"，故游览线形成上下两层，借山登阁，穿洞入穴，上下纵横，游者至此往往

sun shines its radiance on the rockey, its ranges appear more vividly undulating and look more gloriously colorful. Agaianst this background, the rockery, rising steeply from the ground, presents a magnificent view just like that in a painting of a mountain scene in the autumn. The rockery thus becomes a perfect place for a rock climber. Little courtyards, stone bridges and stone shelters are also placed among the rockery. When a visitor walks up and down in the cave by following the man-made scenes, he is totally absorbed by the uniquely enchanting and naturally artificial beauty. When, on top of the hill, he looks afar to the north at the inner and outer city walls with green poplars, he finds Slender West Lake and Pingshan Hall are brought into the garden. To the south of the rockery lies a white mound of rocks that tactfully symbolizes snow, therefore is taken as a scene of winter. Rockeries construct scenes of different seasons when appreciated from different perspectives. Such an effect is achieved only in Yangzhou.

Pavilions and towers are important components in classical Chinese gardens. One is impressed by pavilions and towers which are deliberately placed in disorder and by winding covered walkway reaching high and low. Apart from the outstanding arrangement of water and rocks, gardens in Yangzhou also distinguish themselves by having high and open halls which are usually placed in an important location of a garden. These halls are used to receive visitors and set banquets for them as owners of these gardens are all wealthy merchants who lead a busy social life. The halls are all storied buildings connected by a covered walkway which is in turn double-deckered and thus called "double-deckered walkway". In this way, a visitor may follow two tour routes, one at the upper level and the other at the lower level. He may climb rockeries and ascend pavilions, and walk through holes and into caves. He may, more often than not, lose his directions here having followed the routes upward and downward. This results in the same effect

仿唐南禅寺建筑风格的平山堂鉴真纪念堂
| The memorial hall of Jianzhen at Pingshan Hall built after the style of Nanchan Temple in the Tang Dyanasty

钓鱼台内面面有景
| Charming views from each side of Diaoyu Terrace

个园抱山楼
| Baoshan Tower in Geyuan Garden

个园湖石山夏景
| Lake stone rockeryr in Geyuan Garden in the summe

个园月门春景
| A moon gate in Geyuan Garden in the spring

个园黄石山
| The yellow stone rockery in Geyuan Garden
个园黄石山面西，以石和日照方位来显露秋意。
The yellow stone rockery, facing the west, is indicative of the
autumn with its stones and the slant of sunlight.

个园冬山
| The rockery of winter in Geyuan Garden

迷途，此与苏州园林在平面上的柳暗花明境界有异曲同工之妙。游寄啸山庄，游者必能体会。

寄啸山庄中凿大池，池北楼宽七楹，主楼三间突出，称"蝴蝶厅"。楼旁连复道廊可绕全园，高低曲折，随势凌空。中部与东部又用此复廊分隔，通过上下两层壁间的漏窗可互见两面景色，空透深远。池东筑水亭，四角卧波，为纳凉、演剧之所。在在突出建筑物，而山石水池则点缀其间。洞房曲户，回环四合，隋炀帝在扬州建造迷楼，流风所及，至今尚依稀得之。清乾隆年间《履园丛话》[2]言："造屋之工，当以扬州第一，如作文之有变换，无雷同。虽数间之筑，必使门窗轩豁，曲折得宜。"寄啸山庄使人屡屡难以忘情者，其故在此。

扬州的景物是平处见天真，虽无高山大水，而曲折得宜，起伏有致，佐以婉约轻盈之命名，能于小处见大，简中寓繁，蕴藉多姿。

as demonstrated in gardens in Suzhou, although different approaches are adopted. One will realize this when touring around Jixiao Mountain Resort.

A large pond was dug in Jixiao Mountain Resort. To the north of the pond sites a seven-room wide building, from which stands out the three-room wide main part called Hudie Hall. The side of the building is connected to the double-deckered walkway, winding all the way throughout the garden, sometimes high and sometimes low to adapt to the changing terrain. The covered walkway separates the garden into the middle part and the eastern part. A visitor can enjoy scenes in both parts of the garden through the perforated windows between the two deckers of the covered walkway, thus resulting in views being stretched profoundly deep. To the east of the pond stands a pavilion with its quadrangular eaves corners lying above water. This is an ideal place to enjoy both the cool air in summer and the folk operas in all seasons. Although the buildings are highlighted, rocks and bodies of water are also scattered among them for decoration. Cave rooms, arched doors and rows of houses are built aroumd the garden after the architectural style of Milou Building which was established in Yangzhou by Emperor Yang in the Sui Dynasty. The influential architectural fashion remains vaguely tangible until today. As is put in *Miscellany of Lüyuan Garden*[2] written during the reign of Emperor Qianlong in the Qing Dynasty, "Yangzhou should rank No.1 in the craftsmanship of buildings, for it never repeats itself as exemplified in writings where no sentences are identical. Although a building consists of a small number of rooms, the windows and doors are made high and open in good proportion with curved lines and zigzag shapes." This explains why visitors find their trips to Jixiao Mountain Resort a most unforgettable experience.

The scenery in Yangzhou excels in its purity embedded in plainness. Although there are no lofty rockeries or vast stretch of water, when winding lines and zigzag shapes, deliberately

寄啸山庄园门
| The gate of Jixiao Mountain Resort

寄啸山庄蝴蝶厅
| Hudie Hall in Jixiao Mountain Resort

可绕全园的寄啸山庄复道廊
| The double-deckered walkway winding all the way throughout Jixiao Mountain Resort

小盘谷的九狮山石壁尤为扬州园林中之上选。园中的建筑物与山石、山石与粉墙、山石与水池、前院与后院等配置，利用了幽深与开朗、高峻与低平等对比手法，形成一时间此分彼合的幻景。花墙间隔得非常灵活，山峦、石壁、步石、谷口等的叠置，正是：危峰耸翠，苍岩临流，水石交融，浑然一体。园内虽无高楼奇阁，但幽曲多姿，浅画成图。"以少胜多"的园林设计方法在扬州以此园最具有代表性。

注释：

1. 鉴真（688—763），唐代僧人。自742—753年间六次东渡日本，最后一次成功抵达日本九州南部，后在日本奈良宣讲佛经，759年修建唐招提寺。

2. 《履园丛话》，清钱泳撰，共二十四卷，其中有专门记述园林的文字。

displaced layers and delightful names are brought into the charming and colorful scenario, visitors find gardens being turned spacious on small plots of land, and buildings stylish out of simplistic designs.

　　Jiushishan Rocks in Xiaopangu Garden are among the best in gardens in Yangzhou. The compatible arrangement between buildings and rocks, between rocks and white-washed walls, between rocks and ponds, and between the front yard and the back yard contrasts the serene and open, and steep and plain matching techniques, resulting in an illusionary scenery of seemingly apart, but actually attached. The separating tracery walls are placed so flexibly and the piling of peaks, stone walls, step stones and valley mouths are so skillful that towering peaks amid soaring greens, grotesque rocks surrounded by oozing water are integrated into charmingly harmonious scenery. Although there do not exist any tall buildings or unique pavilions in the garden, it becomes stylish for its scenes being serene and deep, which is as good as a painting composed of just a few lines. "Less is more", the principle guiding garden designs is best represented by this garden in Yangzhou.

Notes:

1. Jianzhen (688-763) was a monk of the Tang Dynasty. He attempted to visit Japan six times from 742 to 753. The last time, he successfully arrived in the southern part of Kyushu, Japan. Later he explained and publicized the Buddhist scriptures in Nara and founded the T ō sh ō dai-ji Temple in 759.

2. *Miscellany of Lüyuan Garden*, written by Qian Yong in the Qing Dynasty, consists of twenty-four volumes, parts of which are on gardens in particular.

扬州小盘谷
| Xiaopangu Garden in Yangzhou

寄啸山庄福寿纹样铺地
| Decorative paving symbolic of happiness and longevity in Jixiao Mountain Resort

寄啸山庄水心亭
| Shuixin Pavilion in Jixiao Mountain Resort

有法无式格自高

园林设计有法而无式，兹据现状，略作具体分析。

江南园林占地不广，然千岩万壑，清流碧潭，皆宛然如画，正如《履园丛话》所说："造园如作诗文，必使曲折有法。"因此，对于山水、亭台、厅堂、楼阁、曲池、方沼、花墙、游廊等的安排，必使风花雪月，光景常新，不落窠臼，始为上品。对于总体布局及空间处理，务使观之不尽，极尽规划之能事。

总体布局可分为以下几种：以水为主题的，其佳构多循"水随山转，山因水活"的基本原则。或贯以小桥，或绕以游廊，间列亭台楼阁，大者中列岛屿，此类如苏州网师园、怡园等。

Elegance Arises from Principles Not Stereotypes

The design of gardens follows principles, not stereotypes. Detailed analyses based on these principles are as follows.

Albeit the limited coverage, the gardens in China south of Changjiang River, picturesque with unique rock formations and clear streams and ponds, are a reflection of the statement in *Miscellany of Lüyuan Garden*: "A garden, just like poetry, should be constructed on principles." That is to say, the ingenious arrangement of rocks and water, pavilions and towers, halls and chambers, ponds and streams, flowerbeds and walkways should present the changing seasonal beauty of nature. The general layout and the utilization of space should be embodied in scenic sights as varied and continuous as possible.

There are different types of layouts. One type of layout uses water for its theme. Classical examples of this type follow the principle of "water flowing around rockeries and rockeries becoming alive because of water". Normally, bodies of water are embellished with bridges over them, covered walkways around them or pavilions and towers near them. Islets are put in the middle of the water in the case of large gardens. Examples of this type include Wangshi Garden and Yiyuan Garden in Suzhou. In contrast, Changyuan Garden at Miaotang Alley, tiny in size, features a pond in the center surrounded by winding covered walkways, presenting a garden as exquisite as potted landscape.

It is crucial for water in a garden to have its sources which keep it from becoming a backwater. For a small garden to impress the visitor with the grandeur of infinity, the key lies in its proper arrangement. Here are two principles to follow. The first one is to choose a plot of irregular land

沧浪亭步碕廊
| Buqi covered walkway in Canglang Pavilion

豫园水上游廊
| A covered walkway above water in Yuyuan Garden

而庙堂巷畅园，地颇狭小，一水居中，绕以廊屋，宛如盆景。

园林之水，首在寻源，无源之水必成死水。然而，园林面积既小，欲使之有汪洋之概，则在于设计得法，其法有二：（一）池面利用不规则的平面，间列岛屿，上贯以小桥，使人望去不觉一览无遗；（二）留心曲岸水口的设计，故意做成许多湾头，望之仿佛有许多源流，如是，则水来去无尽头，有深壑藏幽之感。至于曲岸水口之利用芦苇，杂以菰蒲，则更显得隐约迷离，这要在较大的园林应用才妙。留园活泼泼地水榭临流，溪至榭下势已尽，但亦流入一小部分，俯视之下，若榭跨溪上，水不觉终止。沧浪亭以山为主，但西部的步碕廊突然逐渐加高，高瞰水潭，自然临渊莫测。苏州艺圃和上海豫园之桥与水几平，反之，两岸山石愈显高峻了。怡园之桥虽低于山，似嫌与水尚有一些距离。至于小溪作桥，在对比之下，其情况何如不难想象。古人改用"点其步石"的方法，则更为自然有致。

for a pond which is then laid with islets in it and little bridges over it, presenting an inexhaustible vista. The second one consists in a special design of inlets and outlets of water with curves and forks. In this way, water flows here and there without an end, creating an effect of secrecy and depth. For a larger garden, this effect can be further enhanced by hiding outlets among water plants such as reeds. A good example is Liuyuan Garden in which outlets of a stream are hidden beneath a pavilion by water. Looking down at the water, one is fascinated by the seeming inexhaustibility of the stream which actually comes to an end underneath the pavilion. In the case of Canglang Pavilion which emphasizes the rockery, Buqi covered walkway suddenly rises higher and higher in the western part of the pavilion where when one looks down at the pond, he feels like standing on the edge of an abyss. Bridges in Yipu Garden in Suzhou and Yuyuan Garden in Shanghai are built almost at the same level as the water, thus creating an illusion that the rockeries on both sides are much higher than they really are. However, the bridge in Yiyuan Garden, though at a lower level than the rockery, looks a little too far away from the water. It is not difficult, therefore, to imagine how it looks for bridges to be built over a stream. This is why generations of designers have replaced some of them with stepping rocks, a great improvement towards delicacy and naturalness. Waterfalls are rare except Yanpu Waterfalls in Huanxiu Mountain Resort and in Wangshi Xiaoyuan (Wang's Residence) in the city of Yangzhou.

A designer is more at ease to design a garden with lage stretches of water. Zhuozheng Garden, for instance, has nature-inspired characteristics that in themselves create an atmosphere of infinity and variety. The man-made rockeries in the center and slopes skirting meandering water and beaches make up a more natural landscape. The design of

吴江退思园
| Tuisi Garden in Wujiang

园中厅、房、楼、阁与旱船等建筑排列有序。
Halls, chambers, pavilions, towers and land-boats are placed
in good order in the garden.

南京煦园重檐卷棚歇山顶建筑——夕佳楼
| Xijia Tower—a building with a curved-ridge gable and hip roof with double eaves in Xuyuan Garden in Nanjing

瀑布除环秀山庄、扬州汪氏小苑檐瀑外，他则罕有。

　　基地积水弥漫而占地广，布置遂较自由。如拙政园能发挥开朗变化的特色，其中部的一些小山，平冈小坡，曲岸回沙，都是运用人工方法来符合自然的意趣。池水聚分大小有别，大园宜分，小园宜聚，然聚必以分为辅，分必主次有序。网师园与拙政园是两个佳例，皆苏州园林上品。

　　前水后山，堂筑于水前，坐堂中，穿水遥对山石，而堂则若水榭，横卧波面，苏州艺圃布局即如是。

　　至于中列山水，四周环以楼及廊屋，高低错落，迤逦相续，与中部山石相呼应，如苏州耦园东部者，在苏州尚不多见。

　　其次以山石为全园之主题，如环秀山庄。因该园无水源可得，无洼地可利用，故以山石为主题使其突出，固设计中一法。更略引水泉，俾山有生机，岩现活态，苔痕鲜润，草本华滋，宛然若真山水了。

ponds varies from garden to garden. It is suitable for a large garden to have ponds scattered around the garden and for a small garden to have bodies of water gathered together. The gathered-together ponds are to be complemented by separation whereas scattered-around ponds are to be arranged with a focus. Wangshi Garden and Zhuozheng Garden in Suzhou are two excellent examples in point.

A hall is designed by water, with water flowing in front and rockeries in the back. Similar to a pavilion by water, it looks as if drifting on water. Such a layout is seen in Yipu Garden in Suzhou.

Pavilions and towers of varying heights are also designed around water and rockeries in the center. But this arrangement is rare even in Suzhou with an exceptional case of the eastern part of Ouyuan Garden in Suzhou.

Another type of layout emphasizes rocks and mountains, a theme popular for Chinese gardens. A prime example is Huanxiu Mountain Resort, which, despite the lack of a water source or a depression, successfully achieves a vivid approximation of real mountains with a composition of fresh rock moss with verdant tress and grass, adding a feeling of vitality.

The use of rocks, during the Ming and early Qing Dynasties, emphasizes naturalness with only slight embellishments on existing conditions. Yellow stones from Suzhou, such as those for the two small rockeries in the center of Zhuozheng Garden and those underneath Xiuyi Pavilion are generally used. Though not as exquisitely curved as lake stones, the proper arrangement of yellow stones may turn out a unified entity, neither pretentious nor redundant. Lake stones in large chunks are used extensively in the gardens of the Qing Dynasty to achieve singularity. Gardens

沧浪亭硬山式观音兜山墙屋顶
| The flush gable roof with Guanyindou gable in Canglang Pavilion

煦园石舫不系舟
| Buxizhou, the Stone Boat in Xuyuan Garden

至于用石，明代以至清初园林崇尚自然，多利用原有地形，略加整理。其所用石，在苏州大体以黄石为主，如拙政园中部二小山及绣绮亭下者。黄石虽无湖石玲珑剔透，然掇石有法，反觉浑成，既无矫揉做作之态，又无累石之险。到清代造园，率皆以湖石叠砌，贪多好奇，每以湖石之多少与一峰之优劣与他园计较短长。试以怡园而论，购洞庭山三处废园之石累积而成，一峰一石，自有上选，即其一例。环秀山庄改建于乾隆年间，数弓之池，深溪幽壑，势若天成，其竖石运用宋人山水斧劈皴法，再加镶嵌，简洁遒劲。其水则迂回曲折，山石处处滋润，苍岩欣欣欲活，诚为江南园林的杰构。设计者必须胸有丘壑，叠山造石才可挥洒自如。

掇山既须以原有地形为据，而自然之态又变化多端，无一定成法，不过，自然的形态亦有一定的规律可循。能通乎师造化之理，从自然景物加以分析，证以古人作品，评其妍媸，撷其菁华，当可构成最美的典型。奈何

vie with each other on the amount of lake stones in their decoration and on the merits of a single rock peak. Nevertheless, a thoughtful plan always results in a natural design. Take Yiyuan Garden for example. Rocks from three abandoned gardens near Dongting Mountain were shaped into a magnificent peak. Another example is Huanxiu Mountain Resort, which was renovated during the Qianlong reign. Delicate ponds, deep natural streams and valleys, simple yet vigorous rocks are erected in a style characteristic of the Song Dynasty with winding water moistening the rocks. This is a typical garden in China south of Changjiang River. A designer will be at ease in his layout of piled-up rocks and rockeries when he keeps mountains and valleys in his mind.

Dependence on natural scenery with a variety of forms and styles requires flexibility in design which, nevertheless, is guided by principles, however latent. A designer must make painstaking efforts to study the Creator's law, to observe natural scenes, to appreciate and comment on ancient works and to learn from hard lessons in order to make the classic prototype of gardens. It is a pity that the gardens built in Suzhou in the later periods mainly follow stereotyped patterns with the absence of overall planning. As a result, pavilions, towers, ponds and galleries are pieced together at random. In piling up rocks to build a garden, a peak or a rockery cannot always become as valuable as an antique without the mutual harmony with trees and flowers or complementary integration with buildings. This may well serve as a warning to designers today.

Apart from water, rocks, ponds and depressions, buildings like halls, chambers, terraces, pavilions, towers, galleries, alleys and covered walkways are also major constituents in Chinese gardens. Gardens in China south

网师园内线条优美的飞檐起翘
| The uprising eaves with beautiful curves in Wangshi Garden

苏州所见晚期园林什九已程式化，从不在整体考虑，每以亭台池馆妄加拼凑。尤以掇山造石，皆举一峰片石，视之为古董，对花树的衬托、建筑物的调和等则有所忽略。这是今日园林设计者要引以为鉴的。

中国园林除水、石、池、沼外，建筑物如厅、堂、斋、台、亭、榭、轩、巷、廊等，也是构成园林的主要部分。然江南园林以幽静雅淡为主，故建筑物要轻巧，方始相称，所以在建筑物的地点、平面以及外观上不能不注意。凡园圃立基，先定厅堂景致，"妙在朝南，倘有乔木数株，仅就中庭一二"。江南苏州园林尚守是法，如拙政园远香堂、留园涵碧山房等皆是。至于楼台亭阁的布置，虽无定法，但按基形成，格式随宜，花间隐榭，水际安亭，还是要设计者从整体出发，加以灵活应用。古代讨论造园的书籍如《园冶》《长物志》《工段营造录》等，虽有述及，最后亦指出其不能守为成法。试以拙政园而论，自高处俯视，建筑物虽然是随宜安排，但是其

of Changjiang River are mainly characterized by tranquility and simplicity so much so that buildings are made delicate and exquisite to be agreeable. Consequently, a designer must take the location, the terrain and the outlook into account when designing buildings for his garden. Planning for a garden always starts with the hall, "facing the south, preferably with some arbor trees around just for the main hall". Gardens in Suzhou such as Yuanxiang Hall of Zhuozheng Garden, and Hanbi Mountain Chamber of Liuyuan Garden all follow this rule.

Although there are no set rules on the arrangement of towers, terraces, pavilions and galleries, a designer should give priority to an overall planning and to harmonious integration with the natural terrain, and remain flexible in his layout of towers hidden among flowers and pavilions by the water. Classical works on garden design such as *The Craft of Gardens*, *Superfluous Things* and *Notes of Construction* had discussions about the above-mentioned rules and principles of garden design, but they also made it explicit that these rules and principles should not be followed rigidly. Let us examine Zhuozheng Garden more closely. When looked from above, the buildings in the garden seem to be laid out in a way to fit the natural surroundings; yet they are properly placed to follow certain rules of the direction, both vertically and horizontally. They look largely cheerful with a variety of shapes: squares, rectangles, polygons, and circles, and with a variety of roof patterns: a gable and hip roof, a flush gable roof, an overhanging gable roof, a pyramidal roof, but without a five-ridged roof. A "clay uprising" usually has a low curved modillion that rises up and looks cheerful. Elaborately decorated pendants hanging from the eaves and the slightly bending Wuwang Support all constitute parts of a complete whole. A good example of

豫园小戏台
| A small stage in Yuyuan Garden

豫园
| Yuyuan Garden

豫园的建筑造型非常精致，富有地方色彩。
The buildings in Yuyuan Garden are exquisite in design and
rich in local features.

方向还是直横有序。其外观给人的感觉是以轻快为主，平面正方形、长方形、多边形、圆形等皆有。屋顶形式则有歇山、硬山、悬山、攒尖等，而无庑殿式，且多用"水戗发戗"的飞檐起翘。因此，屋顶外观轻快。檐外玲珑的挂落、柱间微弯的吴王靠，都能取得相互一致的效果。建筑物立面的处理以留园中部而论。自闻木樨香轩东望，对景主要建筑物是曲溪楼，用歇山顶，其外观在第一层做成仿佛台基的形状，与水面相平行的线脚与上层分界，虽系二层，但看去不觉其高耸。尤其曲溪楼、西楼、清风池馆三者的位置各有前后，屋顶立面皆在同中寓不同，与下部的立峰水石都很相称。古木一树斜横波上，益增苍古，而墙上的砖框漏窗、上层的窗棂与墙面虚实的对比，疏淡的花影，都是苏州园林特有的手法，倒影水中，其景更美。明瑟楼与涵碧山房相邻，前者为卷棚歇山，后为卷棚硬山，然两者相联，不能不用变通的办法。明瑟楼歇山山面仅作一面， 另一面用垂脊，

the treatment of the façade can be seen in the central part of Liuyuan Garden. Looking over from Wenmuxixiang Gallery eastward, the main structure in the paired scene is Quxi Tower with a two-layered gable and hip roof. The lower layer of the roof is constructed in the shape of a stage with its edge, parallel to water, as the borderline of the upper layer. As a result, its peak does not look out of proportion, although the roof consists of two layers. In particular, the three buildings of Quxi Tower, West Tower, and Qingfengchi Pavilion are deliberately placed out of order, but their roofs are along a central line and their unique features create a perfect harmony with the towering peaks and lakeside rocks beneath. The uniqueness of Suzhou gardens lies in the old trees that lean over the water, and a nearby wall with brick-framed ornamental perforated windows which strike a sharp contrast with the wall itself, and the pale hue of scattered flowers—all reflected in the water below and creating a multidimensional scene of unsurpassed beauty. Mingse Tower and Hanbi Mountain Chamber, the former with a curved ridge gable and hip roof and the latter with a curved ridge flush gable roof, neighbors to each other, cannot avoid being treated differently, with one of the two facades of Mingse Tower constructed in the usual way, but the other replaced with a vertical ridge, so as to attain a dynamic diversity. In the case of Changyuan Garden whose overly narrow landscape is out of proportion with the pond in the center, making a pavilion by water impossible, and a pavilion with a single gable and hip roof is laid out eventually. In fact, this arrangement follows the same principle mentioned above. In the west, Shuxiao Pavilion and Zhile Pavilion are also examples of disproportion, the former too small to be delicate, and the latter spoiled by its roof whose flowery pattern is so overblown as to be clumsy. In Suzhou, pavilions built in the late

沧浪亭歇山式屋顶
| The gable and hip roof in Canglang Pavilion

寄啸山庄水心亭与复道廊
| Shuixin Pavilion and the double-deckered covered walkway in Jixiao Mountain Resort
水心亭原为园中纳凉、听曲之处，四周环以二层高的复道廊，可使演唱时音响效果更佳。
Shuixin Pavilion used to attract people for retreat from summer heat and for opera singing. A double-deckered covered walkway is built around the pavilion to achieve the best acoustic effect.

不但不觉得其难看，反觉生动有变化。他如畅园，因基地较狭长，中为水池，水榭无法安排，卒用单面歇山，实同出一法。西部舒啸亭、至乐亭，前者小而不见玲珑，后者屋顶虽多变化，亦觉过重，都是比例上的缺陷。江南苏州筑亭，晚近香山匠师每将屋顶提得过高，但柱身又细，整个外观未必真美。反视明代遗构艺圃，屋顶略低，较平稳得多。总之，单体建筑必然要考虑到与全园的整体关系才是。至于平面变化，虽洞房曲户，亦必做到曲处有通，实处有疏。小型轩馆，一间，二间，或二间半均可，皆视基地，位置得当。如拙政园海棠春坞，面阔二间，一大一小，宾主分明。留园揖峰轩，面阔二间半，而尤妙于半间。建筑物的高下得势，左右呼应，虚实对比，在在都须留意。苏州王洗马巷万氏园（原为任氏）虽小，书房部分自成一区，极为幽静，其装修与铁瓶巷任宅东西花厅、顾宅花厅，网师园，西百花巷程氏园，大石头巷吴宅花厅等，都是苏州园林中之上选。怡园旧装修几不

Qing Dynasty lack stability when an exceedingly tall roof is disproportionally supported by notably thin pillars. They are unlike gardens from the Ming Dynasty, whose low roofs are in proportion to the overall layout. In a word, the architectural features must be meticulously designed so that they are integrated and in proportion with each other to form a harmonious whole. To achieve variety in the layout of any given construction, the designer must balance sparseness with density, rounded curves with straight lines, even for buildings with arched doors and curved windows. It is appropriate for a small gallery to have one or two or two and a half spans, as long as it fits in with the natural terrain and is put on a proper location in the garden. For instance, Haitangchunwu of Zhuozheng Garden has two spans, one bigger than the other, with explicitly expressed emphasis. Yifeng Gallery of Liuyuan Garden has two and a half spans with the subtlety of design lying in the half span. It is mandatory that a designer pay close attention to the relativity of height, location, and balance of complexity and simplicity in constructions. The Wan's Garden (formerly Ren's Garden) at Wangxianma Alley in Suzhou is small indeed, but its separate study adds to its tranquility. Its interior decorations along with those found in the West and East Flower Halls of Ren's Residence and the Flower Hall of Gu's Residence at Tieping Alley, in Wangshi Garden, in Cheng's Garden at Xibaihua Alley and in the Flower Halls of the Wu's Residence at Dashitou Alley are all first class among the gardens in Suzhou. Hardly any decorations are left behind of the Yiyuan Garden today, but what is special about the land boats in China south of Changjiang River is their superbly elaborate interior decorations that are well preserved until today.

Covered walkways are as important to gardens as arteries and veins to human bodies.

瞻园亭廊
| A pavilion with a covered walkway in Zhanyuan Garden

以墙分隔的豫园复廊
| Covered double walkways separated by openwork walls in Yuyuan Garden

存，而旱船为江南一带之尤者，所遗装修极精。

园林游廊为园林中的脉络，在园林建筑中处极重要地位。今日苏州园林中常见者为复廊——廊系两面游廊，中隔以粉墙，间以漏窗，使墙内外皆可行走。此种廊大都用于不封闭的园林，如沧浪亭的沿河，或一园中须加以间隔，欲使空间扩大，并使入门有所过渡，如怡园的复廊便是一例，此廊显然仿自沧浪亭。除上述作用外，游廊还可阻朔风与西向阳光。阳光通过廊上漏窗，其图案更觉玲珑剔透。游廊有陆上、水上之分，又有曲廊、直廊之别。造廊忌平直生硬，但过分求曲，亦觉生硬勉强。网师园及拙政园西部水廊小榭，下部用镂空之砖，似为较胜。拙政园旧时柳荫路曲，临水一面栏杆用木制，另一面上安吴王靠，是有道理的。水廊佳者，如拙政园西部的，不但有极佳的曲折，并有适当的坡度，诚如《园冶》所云的"浮廊可渡"，允称佳构。尤其可取的就是曲处湖石芭蕉，配以小榭，更觉有

Nowadays covered double walkways are, more often than not, found in gardens in Suzhou. A double walkway consists of two footpaths separated with a wall in between, ornamented with perforated windows, so that pedestrians can walk on both sides. These covered walkways are mostly found in unfenced gardens, such as the riverside covered walkway in Canglang Pavilion. Double walkways also serve the purpose of landscape division, visual field enlargement, or a preparation at the entrance as exemplified by the double walkway of Yiyuan Garden, obviously built in imitation of the one in Canglang Pavilion. Covered walkways, which also provide shelter from the chill of the wind from the north and the broiling sun from the west elicit an aesthetic appeal when sunlight is screened through the minutely wrought patterns of the ornamental perforations in the windows. Covered walkways differ in their locations and styles—some are on land while others are by water, and some are straight while others are winding. Rigid, straight covered walkways are not recommended because they create a sense of affectation as do excessively crooked walkways. The covered walkways by water and the small pavilions in Wangshi Garden and the western part of Zhuozheng Garden seem to excel with their perforated bricks as supports underneath. In the old days, winding footpaths lay near and far and river banks were lined with green willows in Zhuozheng Garden, so it is reasonable for there to be wooden railings on the side by water and Wuwang Supports on the other side. A fine covered walkway by water, such as the one in the western part of Zhuozheng Garden, has graceful curves and well-designed gradient slopes, just like the walkway mentioned in *The Craft of Gardens* as "a floating cross" which emphasizes its fine structure. The lake stones and plantains at the turning points, supplemented with a small pavilion, generates a sense of variety. Covered walkways over rockeries are mainly used as

沧浪亭回廊
| A winding corridor in Canglang Pavilion

花影入画廊
| Trees and flowers cast shadows on the covered walkway

变化。爬山游廊，在苏州园林中的狮子林、留园、拙政园，仅点缀一二，大都用于园林边墙部分。设计此种廊时，应注意到坡度与山的高度问题，运用不当，顿成头重脚轻，上下不协调。在地形狭宽不同的情况下，可运用一面坡，或一面坡与两面坡并用，如留园西部爬山廊。曲廊的曲处是留虚的好办法，随便点缀一些竹石、芭蕉，都是极妙的小景。李斗[1]云："板上甃砖谓之响廊，随势曲折谓之游廊……入竹为竹廊，近水为水廊。花间偶出数尖，池北时来一角，或依悬崖，故作危槛，或跨红板，下可通舟，递迢于楼台亭榭之间，而轻好过之。廊贵有栏。廊之有栏，如美人服半臂，腰为之细。其上置板为飞来椅，亦名美人靠，其中广者为轩。"言之尤详，可资参考。今日更有廊外植芭蕉，呼为"蕉廊"；植柳，呼为"柳廊"。夏日人行其间，更觉翠色侵衣，溽暑全消；冬日则阳光射入，温和可喜，用意至善。而古时以廊悬画称"画廊"，今日壁间嵌诗条石，都是极好的应用。

side walls or as complementary decorations in Shizilin Garden, Liuyuan Garden or Zhuozheng Garden in the gardens of Suzhou. When designing such a covered walkway, close attention should be paid to the relationship between the gradient and height of a rockery to avoid a top-heavy appearance. In a landscape with a varied width, covered walkways may run along a slope on one side or on one side and on two sides alternatively as in the one winding up a rockery in the western part of Liuyuan Garden. No special efforts have to be made at the turning points of a crooked covered walkway, where such odds and ends as bamboo strips, pebbles or plantains can serve the purpose of creating a simple scene. According to Li Dou[1], "A covered walkway of a wood structure embedded with bricks is called a Xianglang; a covered walkway that winds and undulates with the landscape and serves as a place to take strolls is called a covered strolling walkway... a covered walkway in a bamboo grove is a covered bamboo walkway and a covered walkway by water is a covered water walkway. Tops and corners of buildings are spotted occasionally among trees and flowers and from across a pond. These buildings are erected either by cliffs, or are made look risky, or span on a wood bridge under which boats go along a stream. Covered walkways are built among halls and pavilions and towers, providing easy access among those places. Covered walkways are aesthetically dependent on their railings, which are as good as a short-sleeved dress to reveal partially the bare arms of a lady who has a stylish slender body. Boards are placed on the supports of the railing as flying chairs, known as Beauty's Lazybacks, which mostly appear in covered walkways near galleries." His detailed descriptions of covered walkways may be used for reference. Today there are even covered plantain walkways when plantains are planted beyond the walkway,

拙政园西部水上游廊
| A covered walkway by water in the western part of Zhuozheng Garden

网师园环洞桥
| A small arched bridge in Wangshi Garden

园林中水面之有桥，正如陆路之有廊，重要可知。苏州园林习见之桥，一种为梁式石桥，可分直桥、九曲桥、五曲桥、三曲桥及弧形桥等，其位置有高于水面，与岸相平的，有低于两岸，浮于水面的。以时代面论，后者似较旧，苏州艺圃、怡园，无锡寄畅园及常熟诸园所见的，都是如此。它所表现的效果有二：第一，桥与水平，则游者凌波而过，水益显汪洋，桥更觉其危了；第二，桥低，则山石、建筑愈形高峻，与丘壑、高楼自然成强烈对比。无锡寄畅园假山用平冈，其后以惠山为借景，冈下幽谷间施以是式桥，诚能发挥明代园林设计之高超技术。今日梁式桥往往不照顾地形，不考虑本身大小，随便安置，实属非当，尤其栏杆之高度、形式，都要与全桥及环境作一番研究才是。上选者，如艺圃小桥、拙政园倚虹桥。拙政园中部的三曲五曲之桥，栏杆比例还好，可惜桥本身略高一些。待霜亭与雪香云蔚亭二小山之间石桥仅搁一石板，不施栏杆，极尽自然质朴之意，亦佳

and covered willow walkways with willows by the walkway. Walking through a covered walkway on a summer day, one feels the coolness brought by the green which disperse the summer heat. In winter when the sun shines through leaves, one finds the cozy warmth comforting. In ancient times a covered walkway could be used to display paintings, thus it was called a covered painting walkway, whereas today stone strips with poetic lines are embedded in the walls—an excellent use of the covered walkway.

In a garden, bridges over water are just like covered walkways on land in their importance. Bridges commonly seen in gardens in Suzhou are girder bridges and are classified as straight bridges, bridges of nine turns, bridges of five turns, bridges of three turns and arched bridges. In terms of elevation, some bridges are level with the banks but above the water surface while others sink between the banks and float above the water; in terms of age, the latter are comparatively older such as those in Yipu Garden and Yiyuan Garden in Suzhou, Jichang Garden in Wuxi and gardens in Changshu. Two effect are achieved in these bridges. Firstly, when walking on a bridge that is level with the banks, one feels as if he is stepping on waves. The water seems more thrilling and the bridge really dangerous; secondly, a bridge lower than the banks emphasizes the sharp contrast in height between the bridge and their surrounding rockeries and buildings. An example is Jichang Garden in Wuxi where the rockery is heaped into a flat-topped hillock in front of the background scenery of Huishan Hill, and underneath in the secluded valley are contrasting bridges, all of which display the high standard of garden design in the Ming Dynasty. It is improper for contemporary girder bridges to be casually placed without giving proper considerations to the natural lie of the land nor to its size. Especially

南京瞻园
| Zhanyuan Garden in Nanjing
步石为桥，饶有野趣。
It is of wild fun to cross the stream over step stones.

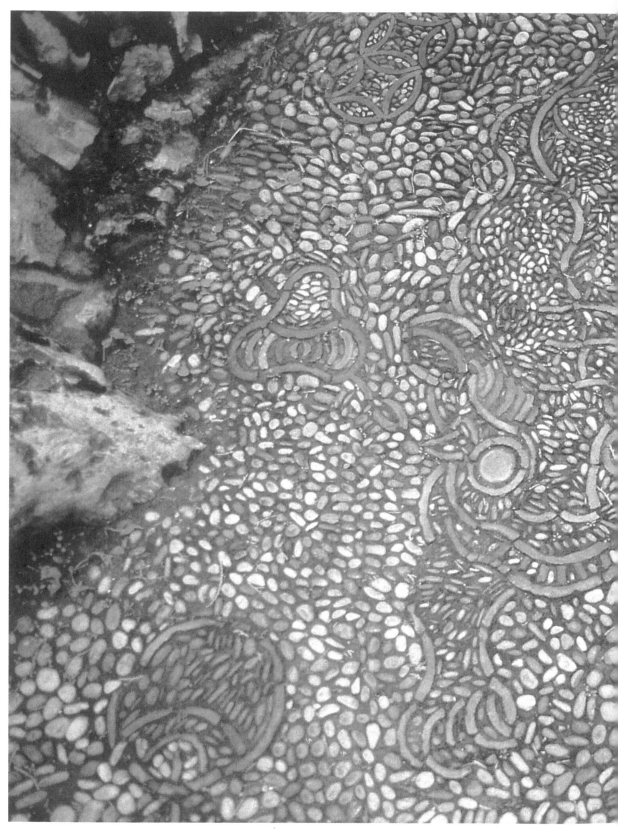

用瓦片卵石侧铺的北海静心斋铺地
| The paving decorated with an animal made of edges of tiles and pebbles in Jingxin Chapel of Beihai Park

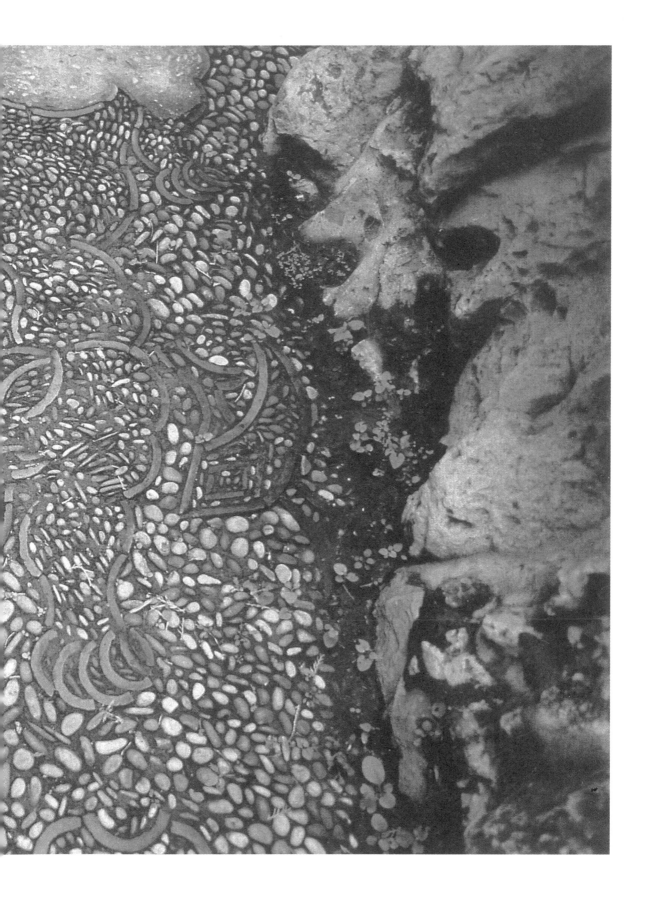

构。苏州园林习见之桥的另一种为小型环洞桥，狮子林、网师园都有。以此二桥而论，前者不及后者为佳，因环洞桥不适宜建于水中部。水面既小，用环洞桥中阻，遂显庞大质实，无空灵之感。网师园之环洞桥建于东部水尽头，桥本身又小，从西东望，辽阔的水面中倒影玲珑，反之，自桥西望，亭台映水，用意相同。至于小溪，《园冶》所云"点其步石"的办法尤能与自然相契合，实远胜架桥其上；可是，此法今日差不多已成绝响了。

《清闲供》云："门内有径，径欲曲。"又云："室旁有路，路欲分。"园林的路，今日我们在苏州园林所见，还能如此。拙政园中部道路，犹守明时旧规，从原来地形出发，加以变化，主次分明，曲折有度。环秀山庄面积小，小路不能不略作迂盘，但亦能恰到好处，有引人入胜之概。然狮子林中道路却故作曲折，悖自然之理，使人莫知所从。

important in the design of railings is the overall management of their height and style relative to the whole bridge. Bridges such as the little bridge in Yipu Garden and Yihong Bridge in Zhuozheng Garden are superbly designed. The railings along the bridge of three turns and bridge of five turns in Zhuozheng Garden are in proportion, but it is a pity to have had the bridges themselves situated a little too high. Between Daishuang Pavilion and Xuexiangyunwei Pavilion is a bridge which is made of just one flagstone and does not have any railings; it is a fine structure that best expresses a natural simplicity. The other type of bridge is a small arched bridge as found in Shizilin Garden and Wangshi Garden. Between the two types, the latter is more preferable than the former, as an arched bridge is not recommended in the middle of ponds. When an arched bridge is situated over a small body of water, the bridge looks large and solid instead of hollow and translucent. The small arched bridge in Wangshi Garden is at the eastern end of a ponds. When one looks to the east from the western end of the bridge, he sees interesting reflections in the vast expanse of water; likewise, when one looks westward form the eastern end of the bridge, he sees the pavilions and towers also reflected in the water. With regard to a brook, the "step stones" used to cross brooks mentioned in *The Craft of Gardens* express a harmony with nature much better than a bridge does. Unfortunately all this seems to have fallen out of favor nowadays.

According to *A Leisurely Country Life*, "a footpath in the courtyard tends to bend"; and "a road beside the house tends to fork". Paths that we see in gardens in Suzhou are just so built. The pathways in the central part of Zhuozheng Garden still remain in the old style of the Ming Dynasty: they bend and turn to highlight the main parts in accordance with the natural features. Because of

瞻园内不同颜色的卵石铺地

| The paving made of colourful pebbles in Zhanyuan Garden

铺地，在园林建设中亦是一件重要的工作，不论庭前、曲径、主路，皆须极慎重考虑。今日苏州园林所见，有侧砖铺于主路，施工简单，拼凑图案自由。碎石地，用碎石侧铺，可用于主路、小径、庭前，上面间有用缸片点缀一些图案。缸片侧铺，间以瓷片，用法同前。鹅子地或鹅子间加瓷片拼凑成各种图案，称"花界"，比上述的要细致雅洁得多，留园自有佳构。冰裂地则用于庭前，其结构有二：其一，即冰纹石块平置地面，如拙政园远香堂前的，颇饶自然之趣，然亦有不平稳的流弊。其二，则冰纹石交接处皆对卯拼成，施工难而坚固，如留园涵碧山房前，极为工整。至于庭前踏跺用天然石叠，如拙政园远香堂及留园五峰仙馆前的，皆饶野趣。

园林的墙，有乱石墙、磨砖墙、漏砖墙、白粉墙等数种。苏州今日所见以白粉墙为最多。外墙有在顶部开漏窗的，内墙间开漏窗及砖框的，所谓"粉墙花影"，为人乐道。磨砖墙，园内仅建筑物上酌用之，园门十之

the small size of Huanxiu Mountain Resort, little paths have to wind up and down the rockery. These winding paths are so designed that they lead to the attractive and fascinating scenery. However, paths in Shizilin Garden are made to wind unnaturally, thus puzzling the visitor with their complexity.

Paving is also important in the garden design. Due attention should be paid to the paving be it for paths in front of the halls, for winding paths or for main roads. In the gardens in Suzhou today, some main roads are built with bricks-on-edge pieced together in a variety of patterns. Gravel is used for other main roads, whereas paths in front of the halls are arranged in a variety of patterns with crockery and china pieces. Patterns using pebbles or a mixture of pebbles and china pieces are known as "Huajie" (colorful land) and are much more delicate and exquisite than those mentioned above, a fine example of which is found in Liuyuan Garden. Paths made of stones veined with crystals are used in front of the halls; they have two types of structures. One type is made of rocks veined with crystals which are laid flat on the ground as on the pathway in front of Yuanxiang Hall in Zhuozheng Garden. This type of pathway has a charming touch of whimsy, but a problem with it is its lack of steadiness. The other type is also made of rocks veined with crystals, but where the rocks meet, they are put in a hooked way. This technique makes the paving process difficult, but the paving is firm and in elegant order as found on the pathway in front of the halls of Hanbi Mountain Resort in Liuyuan Garden. As for the door-steps for halls like those in front of Yuanxiang Hall in Zhuozheng Garden and Wufengxian Pavilion in Liuyuan Garden, they are piled up with stones of natural shapes and therefore are full of wild fun.

Some walls in gardens are made of wild stones of different shapes, polished bricks,

网师园铺地
| The paving in Wangshi Garden
洞门前为碎石铺地，洞门内为侧砖铺地，铺地图案清简。
The paving before the moon gate is made of broken stones, and that
beyond the moon gate is decorated with simple patterns made of the sides
of bricks.

八九贴以水磨砖拼成的图案，如拙政园大门。乱石墙只见于墙的下半部裙肩处。西园以水花墙区分水面，亦别具一格。

对联和匾额为中国园林中不可少的一件重要点缀品。苏州又为人文荟萃之区，当时园林建造亦有文人画家参与，因此山林岩壑，一亭一榭，莫不用极典雅美丽的词句来形容，使游者入其地，览景生情，而这些词句就是这个环境中最恰当的文字描述。例如，拙政园的远香堂和留听阁，同样是赏荷花的地方，前者出自北宋周敦颐"香远益清"句，后者出自唐李商隐"留得残荷听雨声"句。留园的闻木樨香轩、拙政园的海棠春坞，是根据所种的树木来命名的。游者至此，当能体味出许多文学中的境界，这不能不说是中国园林的一个特色。

苏州诸园皆有好的题辞，而怡园诸联集宋词，更能曲尽其意。至于题匾用料，因防园林风大，故十之八九用银杏木阴刻，填以石绿，或用木阴刻后髤漆敷色，色彩都用冷色，亦有

perforated bricks and others are white-washed. Nowadays in Suzhou, white-washed walls are most common. Some external walls have openwork windows at the top whereas internal walls have openwork windows but embedded in brick-frames. These are known as flowery shadows on white-washed walls. Walls of polished bricks are sparingly used for buildings in a garden. Usually, nine out of ten garden gates are embedded in patterns of water-polished bricks such as the gates in Zhuozheng Garden. Walls made of stones of different shapes are only used for the lower parts of walls. In Xiyuan Garden, decorated walls over water are used to separate bodies of water, which is unique indeed.

Couplets and tablets are indispensable decorations used in a Chinese garden. As a habitat of a social and cultural elite, Suzhou has invariably had its gardens built with the collaboration of writers and artists so that everything from a wood to a valley to a single pavilion or a summerhouse bears descriptions in beautiful and elegant language, stimulating the interest of visitors and adding historical value. For example, both Yuanxiang Hall and Liuting Belvedere in Zhuozheng Garden emphasize the traditional appreciation of the lotus; however, they are named after different lines of poetry: the former meaning "fragrant in the distance" is after the line of "getting more delicately fragrant in the distance" by Zhou Dunyi in the Northern Song Dynasty, while the latter meaning "keep to listen to", is after a poem written by Li Shangyin in the Tang Dynasty: "The withered lotuses are kept to listen to the rain as it falls." Wenmuxixiang Gallery in Liuyuan Garden and Haitangchun Yard in Zhuozheng Garden are named after the trees planted there. It is characteristic of Chinese gardens to express an appreciation of Chinese culture and literature.

Inscriptions are interspersed in every garden in Suzhou with Yiyuan Garden displaying the

拙政园香洲文征明所书匾额

| A tablet bearing the characters of *Xiangzhou* inscribed by Wen Zhengming in Zhuozheng Garden

用砖刻的，雅洁可爱。字体以篆、隶、行书为多，罕用正楷，取其古朴自然，与园中景配合方妙。

园林植树，其重要不待细述。苏州园林常见的树种，如拙政园，大树植榆、枫、杨等。留园中部多银杏，西部则漫山枫树。怡园面积小，故植以桂、松及白皮松。尤以白皮松树虽小而姿态古拙，在小园中最显姿态。他则杂以松、梅、棕树、黄杨等生长较为迟缓的树种。此外，园小垣高，阴地多而阳地少，于是墙阴必植耐寒植物，如女贞、棕树、竹之类。岩壑必植松、柏之类乔木。阶下石隙之中，植常绿阴性草类。全园中常绿植物多于落叶植物，则四季咸青，不致秋冬髡秃无物了。至于乔木，若枫、杨、朴、榆、槐、榉、枫等，每年修枝，使其姿态古拙入画。此种树的根部甚美，尤以榆树及枫、杨，树龄大愈老，身空皮留，老干抽条，葱翠如画境。今日苏州园林中之山巅栽树，大致有两种情况：第一类，山巅山麓只植大树，而虚其根部，使可欣赏其根部与山石

richest collection of the enchanting Song poetry. To prevent erosion from strong wind, most of the inscriptions are carved in intaglio on ginkgo wood plates and filled with copper green powder, or carved in intaglio on wood plates and painted, usually in a cold color. Other inscriptions are carved on bricks, which look elegantly clean and delightful. Calligraphic styles of seal characters, clerical scripts and running scripts instead of regular scripts are mostly used because of their stylistic primitive simplicity which matches the natural scenery in a garden.

It goes without saying that planting trees is of vital importance in gardens. A variety are found in gardens in Suzhou such as elm, maple, and poplar in Zhuozheng Garden; in the central part of Liuyuan Garden there are gingko trees and over the rockery in the western part are maples. As Yiyuan Garden covers a relatively small area, cassia, pine, and white bark pine trees are mainly planted there. Of note is the white bark pine tree whose primitive simplicity stands out despite its small size. Other trees found here and there in the gardens are those with slower growth—pine, plum, palm, and box trees. Then, since high walls in these small gardens keep large parts of the landscape in the shade, cold-resistant plants such as privet, palm, and bamboo trees are preferable. Tall trees like pine and cedar planted with big rocks to keep perfect harmony; and evergreen shade-bearing grass is planted in crevices in the rocks or under step stones. Because there are more evergreen plants than deciduous, gardens are green all the year round, thus eliminating the usual emptiness in autumn and winter. Tall trees like hackberry, elm, locust, beech, and maple, which are trimmed every year, are picturesque with simplicity. Exposed roots of these trees are remarkably beautiful, especially those of the elm, maple, and poplar trees, whose trunks become hollow but the barks remain. When the old

豫园龙墙
| The Dragon Wall in Yuyuan Garden
豫园以泥塑、砖刻和墙头雕塑最有名。
Yuyuan Garden is noted for clay and brick carvings as well as wall and
roof sculptures.

之美，如留园与拙政园的一部分。第二类，山巅山麓树木皆出丛竹或灌木之上，山石并攀以藤萝，使望去有深郁之感，如沧浪亭和拙政园的一部分。前者得倪瓒[2]飘逸画意，后者有沈周[3]沉郁之风。至于滨河低卑之地，则种柳、栽竹、植芦，墙阴栽爬山虎、修竹、天竹、秋海棠等。叶翠，花冷，实鲜，高洁耐赏。

园林栽花与植树同一原则。背阴且能略受阳光之地栽植桂花、山茶之类。此二者开花一在秋，一在春初，都是群花未放之时，而姿态亦佳，掩映于奇石之间，冷隽异常。紫藤则入春后，一架绿荫，满树繁花，望之若珠光宝露。牡丹之作台，衬以纹石栏杆，实因牡丹宜高地向阳，兼以其花华丽，故不得不如此。他若玉兰、海棠、牡丹、桂花等同栽庭前，谐音为"玉堂富贵"，虽然命意已不适于今日，但在开花的季节与花彩的安排上，前人未始不无道理的。桃李宜植林，适于远眺，此在苏州，仅范围大的如留园、拙政园可以酌用之。

branches sprout, they create an impressive verdant scene. At present, there are mainly two ways of planting trees on rockeries in Suzhou: the first way being planting big trees only at the top and at foot of a rockery without growing any small plants near them so that people can admire the harmonious beauty between exposed roots and rocks as those seen Liuyuan Garden and Zhuozheng Garden; the second one being planting trees, at the top and foot of a rockery, among clumps of bamboos and bushes, and growing creepers and vines by rocks, giving an impression of greenness, such as that found in Canglang Pavilion and Zhuozheng Garden. The former represents a pursuit of the graceful painting style of Ni Zan[2], while the latter reveals a longing for the melancholy painting nature of Shen Zhou[3]. Willows, bamboos, and reeds grow in the low-lying areas by lakes and rivers, and creepers, bamboos, and begonias in the shade of the nearby walls. These plants bear green leaves, cool flowers, and colorful fruits with superb elegance.

Growing flowers follows the same principle as planting trees. Flowers such as osmanthus and camellias which bloom alternately in autumn and in early spring are planted in shady places that sunshine rarely reaches. These gracefully shaped flowers hidden among the grotesque rocks look usually pretty and tasteful. In spring, the flowers and leaves of the wisteria are like brilliant jewels blotting out the land. Because of people's love for the gracefulness of their blossoms, peonies are traditionally placed on terraces enhanced by marble railings in the background, bathed in sunshine on a high land. Other flowers such as magnolias, crab apples, peonies and osmanthus are planted in front of halls because in the Chinese language, they are collectively homophonic to "Yu Tang Fu Gui" meaning "wealthy and magnificent" which is not really appropriate for the present day though; but the garden design makes much sense

恭王府萃锦园垂花门
| The festooned gate in Cuijin Garden in Prince Gong's Mansion.

植物的布置，在苏州园林中有两个原则：第一，用同一种树，植之成林，如怡园听涛处植松，留园西部植枫，闻木樨香轩前植桂，但又必须考虑到高低疏密及与环境的关系。第二，用多种树同植，其配置如作画构图一样，更要注意树的方向及地势高低是否适宜于多种树性、树叶色彩的调和对比、常绿树与落叶树的配比、开花季节的先后、树叶形态、树的姿势、树与石的关系等，必须要做到片山多致，寸石生情，二者间是一个有机的联系才是。此外，更需注意植物与建筑物的式样、颜色的衬托，是否已做到"好花须映好楼台"的效果。水中植荷，似不宜多。荷多必减少水的面积，楼台缺少倒影，宜略点缀一二，亭亭玉立，摇曳生姿，隔水宛在水中央。据云，昆山顾氏园藕植于池中石板底，石板仅凿数洞，俾不使其自由繁殖。又有池底置缸，植荷其内，用意相同。

江南园林在装修、选石、陈列上极为讲究，而用色则以雅淡为主，

in the arrangement of alternation of blooming seasons and the match of colors. Peaches and plums are planted in groves for enjoyment over a distance, and they are carefully arranged in larger gardens like Liuyuan Garden and Zhuozheng Garden in Suzhou.

Two principles guide the configuration of plants in the gardens of Suzhou. The first dictates trees of the same kind be planted in groves such as the pine tree grove at Tingtao in Yiyuan Garden; the maple tree grove in the western part of Liuyuan Garden; and the osmanthus tree grove in front of Wenmuxixiang Gallery. In doing so, attention must be paid to the interrelationships between the height and density of the trees and their environment. The second principle requires trees of different kinds mixed together to form a picturesque scene. Here attention must be paid to the direction the trees are facing; the blending of the different kinds of trees with the landscape; the contrast and combination of colors; the ratio between evergreen and deciduous trees; the alternation of the blooming periods of the different trees; the shapes of the leaves and of the trees; and the relationship between the trees and rocks. A designer must make every endeavor to build a natural link between rocks and plants so much so that when supplemented with plants a rock may produce scenes of various styles and a stone may stir strong emotions. Attention should also be paid to the coordination of the patterns and colors of the flowers with the surrounding buildings to achieve the effect as described in the line: "stylish flowers to go with stylish buildings." Lotus flowers should not be grown in too much abundance; otherwise, they will reduce the size of the body of water, resulting in fewer reflections of buildings in water. Therefore, only a few slim and graceful lotus plants are needed to create a picturesque scene in the center of a pool. It is recorded that in the garden of the Gu's Residence, lotus flowers are rooted underneath slates with several holes to control the growth. Crocks are

金碧彩绘的恭王府萃锦园小亭
| A splendid pavilion with colorful paintings in Cuijin Garden of Prince Gong's Mansion

这与北方皇家园林的金碧辉煌适成对比。江南住宅建筑所施色彩，在梁、枋、柱头皆用栗色，挂落用墨绿，有时柱头用黑色退光，都是一些冷色调，与白色墙面有着强烈的对比，而花影扶疏，又适当地调和了颜色的对比。且苏州园林皆与住宅相连，为养性读书之所，更应以清静为主。南宗山水画[4]，水墨浅绛，略施淡彩，秀逸天成，早已印在士大夫及文人画家的脑海中。在这种影响下，设计出来的园林当然不会用重彩贴金了。加以江南炎热，朱红等暖色亦在所非宜。这样，园林的轻巧外观，秀茂的花木，玲珑的山石，柔媚的流水，加之灰白的江南天色，都能相互匹配并调和，予人的感觉是淡雅幽静。

中国园林还有一个特色，就是不论风雨晦明，在各种环境下，都能景色咸宜，予人不同的美感。如夏日的蕉廊、荷池，冬日的梅影、雪月，春日的繁花、丽日，秋日的红蓼、芦塘，虽四时之景不同，而景物无不适人。

said to be placed at the bottom of the pond in which to plant the lotuses, another way to serve the same purpose.

The designers of gardens in China south of Changjiang River are extremely particular about the decorations and rock selections used in a layout, for they like to emphasize soft light colors that have a gentle and simple appeal. This is in sharp contrast to the splendid and magnificent royal gardens in the north. The beams, crossbeams, and column caps of residences in China south of Changjiang River are maroon in color and hanging fascias are greenish black. Sometimes the column caps are matted with a black color or other similar cool colors to form a sharp contrast with the white walls with scattered flowers used to soften the contrast. Serenity is the main consideration of building gardens in Suzhou, for the culture of the mind is the purpose of gardens. The avoidance of heavy colors is an influence from the landscape paintings of the Southern School[4]. And moreover, warm colors do not go well with the warm climate in China south of Changjiang River. In this way, the deft outlook, luxuriant plants, exquisite rocks, gentle rivers and the gray-white sky of China south of Changjiang River all fit well into an excellent frame, giving an impression of simplicity, elegance and tranquility.

Another characteristic of Chinese gardens is that even in inclement weather, they remain beautiful and inviting. Although the variation of the scenery from season to season never fails to appeal: the covered plantain walkways and lotus pools in summer; the plum blossoms and snowflakes in winter, the colorful flowers and sunny days in spring; and the Polygonum orientale and reed ponds in autumn. This is how scenes as Wind Sounds Through Pine Waves, A Lonely Cattail in Rain, Shadows of Flowers in Moonlight and Pavilions Lost in Fog come into effect. Such scenarios result chiefly from artistic

淡淡江南三月天
| The sky of March in China south of Changjiang River

故有"松风听涛""菰蒲闻雨""月移花影""雾失楼台"等景致。造景来达到这些效果，主要在于设计者有高度的文学艺术修养，使理想中的境界付之于实现，如对花影要考虑到粉墙，听风要考虑到松，听雨要考虑到荷叶，月色要考虑到柳梢，斜阳要考虑到漏窗，岁寒要考虑到梅竹，等等。安排一石一木，都寄托了丰富的情感，使得处处有情，面面生意，含蓄曲折，余味不尽。

注释：

1. 李斗，清代文人，生卒年不详，著有《扬州画舫录》，其中有专章记述扬州园林的文字。

2. 倪瓒（1301 或 1306—1374），元朝大画家，擅画水墨山水，自谓"逸笔草草，不求形似"，"聊写胸中逸气"。其"简中寓繁，似嫩实苍"的画风对造园颇多启发。

3. 沈周（1427—1509），明朝画家，擅画山水，取景江南山川和园林景物，其画多具园林意境。

4. 唐代，中国山水画开始盛行，有李思训父子着色山水及王维的写意、渲染画风。至明代，董其昌始议分南北二大宗派之说，并对南宗水墨写意推崇备至。

ideals materialized into the reality. All of these vistas are taken into consideration: the relationship of the shadows of flowers against white-washed walls; the sound of the wind blowing in through the pine trees; the ticktack sound of rain drops falling on lotus leaves; the brilliance of the moon illuminating the willow branches; the light of the setting sun perforating through lattice windows; and the year-end chill incapable of intimating the plum blossom and bamboos. Even the arrangement of a rock or tree is saturated with rich sentiments.

Notes:

1. Li Dou, a man of letters in the Qing Dynasty (dates of birth and death unidentified), was the author of *Records of Pleasure Boats of Yangzhou* which describes gardens in Yangzhou in a chapter.

2. Ni Zan (1301 or 1306-1374) was a great painter of the Yuan Dynasty who was good at painting landscapes. He described his paintings as being completed "with free and casual strokes, and not restricted by shapes of objects" and "just to express my free mind". His painting style of "complexity embedded in simplicity" and "sophistication embedded in immaturity" has great influence upon the garden design.

3. Shen Zhou (1427-1509) was a painter of the Ming Dynasty. He was good at painting landscapes, especially mountains and water and gardens in China south of Changjiang River. Therefore, most of his paintings were completed with artistic motifs of gardens .

4. Landscape paintings were gaining popularity in the Tang Dynasty with leading painters such as Li Sixun and his son who painted landscapes in color and Wang Wei who developed a painting style of freehand brushwork and applying colors to paintings. In the Ming Dynasty , Dong Qichang advocated two schools for the classification of different styles in painting: a southern school and a northern school; and he was an ardent supporter of the southern school of freehand wash painting.

春到庭园

| Spring in the yard

后记 | Afterword

前岁丧妻，去年哭子，颓唐老境，排忧无从，唯"以园为家，以曲托命"，终日徘徊周旋于泉石歌管间，解我何人？是稿前数年作也，兴移随笔，非为述著，亦聊志触景之所感耳。见仁见智，未必强求人同，存一家之说而已。流年逝水，花落鸟啼，今日视之，顿同隔世矣。

园林贵自然，记园之文亦宜然，其理一也。小颓风范，丘壑独存。乱头粗服，未失真相。无心藻饰，倦意增修。草草付梓，颇能见真情也。过眼行云，动人幽思，从古几人省。兹方余营上海豫园东部成，与此书之刊出，留鸿爪于雪泥，听雅曲于园林，余愿已足。此记之所以赘言也。秋月当窗，怀人天际，虫声四壁，搁笔凄然。

陈从周
于豫园谷音洞之南轩

I lost my wife the year before last year, and I lost my son last year. Being old and dispirited, there was no way for me to escape from the hollowed sadness but to "indulge myself in gardens and save my life with music". I lingered around the streams and stones amid melancholy tunes, but who could take me out? I composed the scripts several years ago just to note down my personal interest as records of my reflections upon the scenes, but not to write a book for publication. As different people have different opinions, I expressed my own personal opinions here with no intent to attract agreement with me. Time flows away like water, as followers wither and birds weep. It seemed to have depicted a different world when I read the scripts again today.

The essence of a garden lies in its naturalness, so do writings of the garden. They both follow the same principle. A man may no longer have perfect manners, but the hills and valleys in his heart remain unchanged; my nature remained unchanged though I was in plain clothes with hair untrimmed. My true feelings were conveyed albeit the scripts were submitted without revisions for I did not intent to polish the scripts. Clouds floated by and stirred peple's heart; but how many people reflected upon them? This book was published upon completion of the restoration project of the eastern part of Yuyuan Garden in Shanghai which I led, I was satisfied for having left my humble footprints on a snow path and appreciated tuneful music in gardens, This postscript was, therefore, something unnecessary. With moonlight of autumn shining into my windows, and crickets chirping through the walls, I put down my pen in sadness, lost in memory of my beloved in heaven.

Chen Congzhou
at Nanxuan Chamber by Guyin Valley in Yuyuan Garden